BRITISH RAIL IN THE 1980s AND 1990s
ELECTRIC LOCOMOTIVES, COACHES, DEMU AND EMUs

Kenny Barclay

T0293901

AMBERLEY

Dedicated to my wonderful mother Elizabeth Barclay, who spent many long hours reading over my draft work of this and my previous books. Your knowledge of road and rail transport within Britain during the 1980s and 1990s will be greatly improved. All your hard work and support is greatly appreciated.

First published 2018

Amberley Publishing
The Hill, Stroud
Gloucestershire, GL5 4EP

www.amberley-books.com

Copyright © Kenny Barclay, 2018

The right of Kenny Barclay to be identified as the Author of this work has been asserted in accordance with the Copyrights, Designs and Patents Act 1988.

ISBN 978 1 4456 7021 8 (print)
ISBN 978 1 4456 7022 5 (ebook)

British Library Cataloguing in Publication Data.
A catalogue record for this book is available from the British Library.

Origination by Amberley Publishing.
Printed in the UK.

Foreword

During my time with British Rail I spent various years as a passenger guard and as a passenger driver before moving to driver manager grades in Southern Region. I spent time at Slade Green where the depot was moving out of British Rail management and getting ready for privatisation with Network SouthEast leading on this program. During the late '80s it was exciting times in the south with large change projects taking a lot of everyone's time, including, to name a few: the Trainman concept, wherein the future recruitment of drivers was to come from the Trainmen (D) grades; the early '90s was to see driver-only operation (DOO) introduced across all suburban routes; and the phasing out of slam-door rolling stock and the introduction of the Class 465/466 Networkers on all suburban areas.

As British Rail was gradually broken up and privatised, the first franchise was offered out to a French owner, with Connex being the preferred bidder. Connex also went on to manage South Central, so there were opportunities open for people to gain experience with a sister operator locally in the south. I gained very valuable management experience during these times with lots of new projects being introduced in short time scales very successfully.

Perry Ramsey
Operations Director, Scotrail Alliance

Introduction

The first electrified railway line in Britain was Volk's Electric Railway, which opened in 1883 along the seafront in Brighton and is still in operation today. The line, which is just over 1 mile long, was originally electrified at 50 V DC. This was later increased to 140 V DC and now it operates at 110 V DC from a third rail supply. In 1921 the British government decided that 1,500 V DC delivered through overhead wires would be the national standard for electrification. Very few lines were actually electrified at this voltage with one notable line being the Woodhead line between Manchester and Sheffield, which opened in 1953. The line closed to passengers in 1969 with some of the withdrawn 1,500 V DC locomotives seeing further service in the Netherlands. The line closed completely in 1981, at which point much of the overhead electrification equipment was removed.

Currently, most electrified lines south of London are electrified by way of a third rail supplying a 750 V DC current. The first South London suburban electrification using this method was completed before the First World War on lines from London Waterloo station. Third rail electrification continued before and after both world wars to steadily increase the area covered, with the final large-scale project being the electrification to Weymouth in 1988. During the sectorisation period Network SouthEast also completed a number of infill electrification schemes, leaving just a few non-electrified lines. Initially a 660 V DC supply was used for third rail lines, but this was later changed to 750 V DC, which is the current standard. The future of the third rail network is unsure with both Network Rail and the ORR (Office of Road & Rail) stating that 750 V DC third rail lines have a limited future as trains become increasingly power hungry and the 750 V DC lines consequently struggle to cope. In the future some third rail electrified lines may be converted to 25 kV AC overhead electrified lines. Lines around the Merseyside area are also currently electrified using the 750 V DC third rail system.

In 1956 British Rail decided that all future electrification outwith the current third rail electrified areas would be 25 kV AC, delivered via overhead wires. The first major project to use the 25 kV AC system was the electrification of the West Coast Main Line between 1959 and 1974. This project saw local lines around the Birmingham, Liverpool, Manchester and Glasgow areas also being electrified. Later, many lines to the north of London and in the Glasgow area that had previously been electrified using overhead wires at just 6.25 kV AC due to the number of overhead bridges and tunnels were gradually converted to 25 kV AC lines, which was made possible through the fitting of improved insulators. The last of these lines were converted in the 1980s.

Following electrification of the West Coast Main Line in 1974, the East Coast Main Line was then electrified between 1975 and 1991. The electrification was carried out in two stages, with London Kings Cross to Royston being completed between 1975 and 1978 and the section between Royston and Edinburgh, including Leeds, being completed between 1984 and 1991. The Midland Main Line was also electrified between London St Pancras and Bedford in 1983.

Other notable electrification expansion projects around this time saw overhead wires extend to Stanstead Airport in 1990 and Heathrow Airport in 1994. In 1988 the Thameslink line opened between Bedford in the north and Brighton in the south. The line operates over both 25 kV AC and 750 V DC electrified lines. New dual-voltage Class 319 units were ordered to operate over this line.

In 2006, approximately forty per cent – or just over 3,000 miles – of Britain's railway lines were electrified by either 25 kV AC overhead wires (64 per cent) or 750 V DC third rail supply (36 per cent).

Electrification is expanding with parts of the Great Western Main Line currently being electrified and there are further plans to hopefully expand the electrification of the Midland Main Line. However, the recent economic downturn has resulted in many planned electrification projects being either scaled back or put on hold.

Within Scotland the electrification of many major lines across the Central Belt, including the main route between Glasgow and Edinburgh via Falkirk, is currently underway. The first electric trains are due to begin operating between Glasgow Queen Street and Edinburgh Waverley station by early 2018. This follows on from modest extensions over the past few years to the existing electrified Scottish network, much of which dates from the 1960s.

This book follows on from my earlier publication, entitled *British Rail in the 1980s and 1990s: Diesel Locomotives and DMUs,* and turns the attention to focus on the electric locomotives, coaching stock, DEMU and EMU vehicles operating throughout Britain in the 1980s and 1990s. These were interesting and colourful times for the railways of Britain; after years of being formed into regions and with rolling stock being painted either blue or blue and grey, BR restructured itself into business sectors. Electrification was expanding, and many new electric locomotives and EMUs were being delivered to operate over the newly electrified lines. The changes were fast-paced and ultimately prepared British Rail for the privatisation process that began in 1994.

All the photographs within this book are my own work, having been captured over many years with my trusty Canon AE1 camera. At the time the photographs were taken, I was employed by British Rail. I enjoyed the privilege of free staff travel and was therefore able to travel around the network, recording the many changes. I was also fortunate in that I was able to gain access to a number of depots and works around the country, where I could again photograph the changes. I hope you enjoy this small selection that I have chosen from my collection as much as I have enjoyed compiling this volume.

Kenny Barclay
October 2017

Class 73 Locomotive No. 73001

Between 1962 and 1967, forty-nine Class 73 locomotives were constructed. The first six locomotives were built by BR at Eastleigh Works in 1962 and the next forty-three locomotives were constructed by English Electric between 1965 and 1967 at English Electric's Vulcan Foundry. No. 73001 entered service as E6001 on 1 February 1962 and spent many years operating over the Southern Region, later becoming No. 73001. In June 1993 she moved to Birkenhead North Depot to operate for Merseyrail and was later repainted into Merseyrail's yellow livery and was renumbered 73901. She was finally withdrawn in May 2000 and happily lives on in preservation as part of the Dean Forest Railway, wearing BR blue livery. No. 73001 is pictured resting between duties at Stewarts Lane Depot, London.

Class 73 Locomotive No. 73002

No. 73002 is pictured wearing BR blue large logo livery at Stewarts Lane Depot, London. She was new to traffic as E6002 in March 1962 following construction by BR at Eastleigh Works. She would later receive number 73002 and in June 1993 passed to Merseyrail at Birkenhead North Depot for shunting and departmental duties. She is recorded as being withdrawn in June 1995 and has been in long-term storage at the Dean Forest Railway, still wearing BR blue large logo livery.

Class 73 Locomotive No. 73004

New to traffic as E6004 in July 1962, she later received number 73004 under the TOPS renumbering. Between 1987 and 1990 she carried the name *The Bluebell Railway*. She is pictured wearing Network SouthEast blue livery complete with yellow cab sides at Stewarts Lane Depot, London. She was withdrawn in September 1991 and later passed to Merseyrail's Birkenhead North Depot to provide spare parts for sister locomotives. After many years in storage she was finally scrapped by the Harry Needle Railroad Company at EMR Kingsbury in February 2004.

Class 73 Locomotive No. 73005

Pictured wearing Network SouthEast blue livery inside Stewarts Lane Depot, London, No. 73005 was new to traffic as E6005 in August 1962. She carried the name *Mid Hants Watercress Line* between August 1988 and August 1993 and in June 1993 she passed to Merseyrail, with whom she was based at Birkenhead North Depot. After a period in preservation she was converted to a Class 73/9 locomotive. This conversion involved, among other modifications, the removal of the 600 hp engine, which was replaced with a MTU 1,600 hp V8 engine. She received fleet number 73966 and as part of the GB Railfreight fleet she now operates services for the Caledonian Sleeper.

Class 73 Locomotive No. 73105

No. 73105 was new to traffic in December 1965 as E6011. She was part of the second batch of Class 73 locomotives that were constructed between 1965 and 1967 by English Electric at their Vulcan Works. She is pictured wearing Civil Engineers 'Dutch' grey with yellow band livery, which she continued to carry during her time in preservation. She carried the name *Quadrant* between 1987 and 1990. After being withdrawn she entered preservation like many other Class 73 locomotives and from 2003 spent many years in storage. In 2014 her years of storage were over when she was moved to Brush, Loughborough, for conversion to a Class 73/9. Now back in main line service wearing the Caledonian Sleeper livery, she carries fleet number 73969.

Class 73 Locomotive No. 73107

Pictured wearing original InterCity livery at Stewarts Lane Depot, London, No. 73107 was new as E6013 in December 1965. Over the years she has carried three different names, including the same name twice. Between April 1994 and June 2004 and again from September 2010 until July 2015 she carried the name *Redhill 1844 – 1994*. From September 2004 until August 2010 she was named *Spitfire* and finally, in August 2015, she was named *Tracy*. After her InterCity duties were finished she received Civil Engineers 'Dutch' grey with yellow band livery, but by 2000 she was in storage at Old Oak Common Depot, London. She is now owned by GB Railfreight and carries standard GB Railfreight blue livery.

Class 73 Locomotive No. 73126

New to traffic in May 1966 as E6033, she later received fleet number 73126. Between 1991 and 1997 she carried the name *Kent & East Sussex Railway*. She is pictured wearing Network SouthEast livery at Ashford station on 6 June 1992 while hauling a charter train consisting of Class 423/4 4VEP unit No. 3449 as part of the Ashford Chart Leacon Depot open day event. She was officially withdrawn in January 1999 and moved to the Fire Service Training College in Moreton-in-Marsh for use in training exercises. She is recorded as being scrapped by CF Booths, Rotherham, in August 2009.

Class 73 Locomotive No. 73136

No. 73136 is pictured undergoing maintenance inside Stewarts Lane Depot, London, and is wearing departmental grey livery. She entered service in September 1966 as E6043 and has carried three names to date. Between 1992 and 2004 she was named *Kent Youth Music* followed by *Perseverance* between 2005 and 2015. Finally, in August 2015, she received the name *Mhairi*. She holds the honour of being the last Class 73 locomotive to be withdrawn by EWS Railways and upon withdrawal she was purchased by the Class 73 locomotive Preservation Company. The company was renamed Transmart Trains in 2010 and in 2013 sold No. 73136 to GB Railfreight. Locomotive No. 73136 is now based at St Leonards Depot and is an active member of the GB Railfreight fleet.

Class 73 Locomotive No. 73205

Locomotive No. 73205 entered service in May 1966 as E6031. Under TOPS she became No. 73124 and carried this number until February 1988 when she then became No. 73205. She was renumbered again in March 2014 when she became No. 73964 after conversion to a Class 73/9 locomotive. She is pictured wearing Mainline livery at Ashford Chart Leacon Depot open day on 6 June 1992. She is pictured next to a Class 33 locomotive, No. 83301, and at this time both locomotives were being used for testing Eurostar bogies. The testing consisted of providing power from the third rail via Eurostar bogies that had been fitted to the Class 33 to locomotive No. 73205 at speeds up to 90 mph. After a period in storage for much of 2010 she returned to service in 2011, outshopped in InterCity Executive livery.

Class 73 Locomotive No. 73208

No. 73208 is pictured at London Victoria station while operating a Gatwick Express service. At the time Gatwick Express services were operated in push-pull mode with a Class 73 at one end of the train and a converted former Class 414 2HAP motor vehicle, known as a Class 489 GLV vehicle, at the opposite end. She was new to traffic in April 1966 as E6028 and would later carry fleet number 73121 until being renumbered 73208 in February 1988. In June 2014 she was renumbered again to 73965 as part of her conversion to a Class 73/9 locomotive. Between 1983 and 1999 she carried the name *Croydon 1883 – 1983* and on 10 June 2006 she was named *Kirsten* at London Victoria station. She is now an operational member of the GB Railfreight fleet and wears the company's blue and yellow livery.

Class 73 Locomotive No. 73212

Pictured inside Stewarts Lane Depot, London, No. 73212 is wearing InterCity livery. The 73A depot plaque fitted to the front of the locomotive denotes Stewarts Lane Depot. She was new as E6008 in October 1965 and later received fleet number 73102 before being renumbered to 73212 in February 1988. By 1994 she had been repainted into InterCity Gatwick Express livery, and then, after the introduction of new rolling stock, she passed with sister locomotive No. 73213 to Railtrack. Later she then passed to First GBRF and received the company's blue livery. She is now the oldest Class 73 still in service and as part of the GB Railfreight fleet she carries the current GB Railfreight blue and yellow livery.

Class 81 Locomotive No. 81005

When British Rail ordered its first AC electric locomotives for the newly electrified West Coast Main Line, they decided to split the order for the 100 locomotives between five different companies. Twenty-five Class 81 locomotives were delivered between 1959 and 1964. The order was placed in 1959 with BTH (British Thomson-Houston), with construction being carried out at the Smethwick Works of the Birmingham Railway Carriage & Wagon Company. No. 81005 was delivered as E3006 in July 1960 and is pictured shunting at London Euston station in BR blue livery. She is recorded as being withdrawn in February 1989 and after a short period in storage at Crewe Electric Depot she was scrapped in November 1991 by Coopers Metals, Sheffield.

Class 81 Locomotive No. 81017

Locomotive No. 81017 was new to traffic in April 1961 as E3020. She is pictured inside Willesden Depot, London, and again is wearing BR blue livery. The Class 81 locomotives were known as AL1 locomotives. As newer AC locomotives were delivered, many Class 81 locomotives were withdrawn, and by 1989 only a handful remained. Locomotive No. 81017 was one of the last two Class 81 locomotives in service and both No. 81017 and No. 81012 were withdrawn in July 1991. Like many other Class 81 locomotives she was scrapped by Coopers Metals, Sheffield, in November 1991.

Class 82 Locomotive No. 82008

The second type of AC electric locomotives ordered for the West Coast Main Line were the Class 82s, designated AL2. A total of ten were ordered from the Metropolitan Vickers Company. Construction was carried out by Beyer-Peacock at their Gorton Works, Manchester, with locomotive No. 82008 being constructed in 1961 and entering service numbered E3054. The Class 82 locomotives were the most powerful of the five types ordered by BR (AL1–AL5). After final withdrawal in 1987, locomotive No. 82008 was stored with many other early AC locomotives at Crewe until she was bought in 1993 for preservation. She is pictured attending an open day event at Crewe Depot on 3 May 1997. She remains in preservation today as part of the AC Locomotive Group's collection and is currently painted in original InterCity livery.

Class 83 Locomotive No. 83012

The Class 83 locomotives were manufactured by English Electric at Vulcan Foundry, Newton-le-Willows, between 1960 and 1962. Fifteen locomotives were ordered and they were known as AL3 locomotives. When first introduced the Class 83 locomotives suffered from reliability issues and in 1969 the locomotives were placed into storage. The extension of the WCML electrification to Glasgow saw the Class 83 locomotives being refurbished at Doncaster Works before returning back into service. No. 83012 entered service on 8 July 1961 as E3035. She was withdrawn from front line service in 1983 and was relegated to empty coaching stock moves between London Euston station and Wembley Depot until 1988. She is pictured at London Euston station in Mainline livery and retains her four digit headcode box and 'cross-arm pantograph'.

Class 84 Locomotive No. 84001

An order for ten Class 84 locomotives, designated AL4 locomotives, was placed with the North British Locomotive Company, Glasgow, with the first locomotives entering service in March 1960. No. 84001 was new to traffic in March 1960 as E3036. Being constructed at Springburn, Glasgow, meant that many of the Class 84 locomotives underwent testing on the electrified Glasgow suburban lines. She remained in service until January 1979, at which point she was repainted and loaned to the National Railway Museum at York, where this photograph was taken. After many years in open storage she passed to the AC Locomotive Group and moved to Barrow Hill Roundhouse.

Class 85 Locomotive No. 85037

The Class 85 locomotives were originally designated as AL5 locomotives and were the final class that formed part of the first 100 AC electric locomotives. The Class 85 locomotives were constructed by BR at Doncaster Works between 1961 and 1964. In total forty Class 85 locomotives were constructed and featured a power rating of 3,200 hp with a top speed of 100 mph. During a test run a Class 85 managed to record a speed of 119 mph. locomotive No. 85037 is pictured at Crewe station and was new to traffic as E3092 in February 1964. Withdrawal came in September 1990 and she was then stored at Crewe Electric Depot with many others until being scrapped by MC Metals, Springburn, Glasgow, in October 1992.

Class 85 Locomotive No. 85037

Another view of locomotive No. 85037, but this time taken at Warrington Bank Quay station. The Class 85 locomotives featured AEI traction equipment similar to the Class 81 locomotives built by the Birmingham Railway Carriage & Wagon Company. Withdrawal for the class began in earnest in 1989 and all except No. 85101, which was saved for preservation, were withdrawn by 1991.

Class 85 Locomotives No. 85101

No. 85101 was new into service as E3061 on 23 December 1961. In 1974 she received fleet number 85006 before becoming the first Class 85/1 in 1989, consequently being renumbered 85101. Happily, No. 85101 lives on after being secured for preservation in 1993. She was later acquired by the AC Locomotive Group in 1997 and shortly after she underwent an extensive restoration, emerging wearing Railfreight Distribution livery. She is pictured on 27 July 2003 at Doncaster Works, where she was constructed in 1961, taking part in an open day event to celebrate 150 years of Doncaster Works. In August 2013 she regained her fleet number 85006 and was repainted back into BR blue livery.

Class 85 Locomotive No. 85109

Pictured resting between duties at Carlisle station, No. 85109 wears BR blue livery. She was new to traffic as E3090 in October 1963 and she later received fleet number 85035 before becoming 85109 in June 1989. In 1989, due to the late delivery of Railfreight Distribution's Class 90 locomotives, fourteen Class 85 locomotives were modified to become Class 85/1 locomotives. This included the removal of the locomotives' ETH supply and restricting the maximum speed to 80 mph. Although all fourteen of the Class 85/1 locomotives were allocated to Railfreight Distribution, none received Railfreight Distribution livery. No. 85109 was withdrawn from service in 1991 and is recorded as being scrapped by MC Metals, Springburn, Glasgow, in October 1992.

Class 86 Unidentified Locomotive

For the next 100 AC locomotives BR ordered just one class, the Class 86. The first forty were constructed by BR at their Doncaster Works and the next sixty were constructed by English Electric at their Vulcan Foundry Works, Newton-le-Willows. Originally designated AL6 locomotives, they first entered service in August 1965. In this photograph an unidentified Class 86 is pictured wearing early InterCity livery while passing through Pollokshields East station, south Glasgow. This was a diversionary route for InterCity services and it can be assumed the West Coast Main Line was closed for engineering work between Newton and Glasgow Central on the day the photograph was taken.

Class 86 Unidentified Locomotive

Another unidentified Class 86 locomotive is this time pictured inside BRML Springburn Works. She will emerge wearing full InterCity livery as carried by many Class 86 locomotives around this time. The Class 86 locomotives featured axle-hung traction motors. When first introduced into service, the increased unsprung weight within the axles caused damage to the tracks when running at high speeds. In 1969, locomotive E3173, which would become No. 86204, was fitted with flexicoil suspension to improve ride quality and, more importantly, to prevent damage to the track. The modification was a success and, beginning in 1971, all other Class 86 locomotives were converted. Locomotives without the flexicoil springs were restricted to 80 mph until converted.

Class 86 Locomotive No. 86205

No. 86205 was constructed in November 1965 at BR Doncaster Works and entered service shortly after, numbered E3129. Between October 1979 and November 2003 she carried the name *City of Lancaster*. In September 1988 she was one of eight Class 86/2 locomotives to become freight-only locomotives and during this time she carried the number 86503 before reverting back to No. 86205 in November 1990. In this photograph she is pictured in full InterCity livery, passing through the city she was named after. In July 2009 she became No. 86701 and received a red and grey livery, and, carrying the name *Orion*, she was used for ice-breaking duties. She has now left the UK and operates freight services for Bulmarket in Bulgaria, carrying fleet number 85001.

Class 86 Locomotive No. 86214

New as E3106 after construction in June 1965 at BR Doncaster Works, No. 86214 is pictured in InterCity livery at the head of a train at Glasgow Central station. As can be seen in the photograph, Platform 3 is not particularly long and the train is over length for the platform. She was named *Sans Pareil* in April 1980, meaning 'without equal' in French, and was named after the steam locomotive built by Timothy Hackworth that carried the same name. In 1980 she received a special livery to commemorate the 150th anniversary of the Liverpool & Manchester Railway. She was withdrawn in October 2002 still wearing her InterCity livery and is recorded as being scrapped by Ron Hill, Rotherham, in March 2006.

Class 86 Locomotive No. 86222

No. 86222 was constructed by BR Doncaster Works in December 1965 and entered service numbered E3131. In 1989 she was one of eight Class 86/2 locomotives to be transferred briefly to the Railfreight sector and received fleet number 86502. At this time she received Railfreight Distribution livery and had her top speed reduced to 75 mph. Upon her return to the InterCity sector she gained InterCity livery and is pictured as such attending an open day event at Manchester Longsight Depot on 26 April 1992. She is recorded as being withdrawn from service in October 2002, by which time she carried Virgin Trains livery. She was scrapped at Immingham in December 2003.

Class 86 Locomotive No. 86239

No. 86239 was one of sixty Class 86 locomotives constructed by English Electric and entered service as E3169 in June 1965. She briefly became a freight-only locomotive numbered 86507 between December 1988 and July 1989 and carried Railfreight two-tone grey livery. She was named *L. S. Lowry* in October 1980 after the famous Manchester artist. Sadly, No. 86239 was involved in a fatal accident at Stafford on 8 March 1996. She was withdrawn after the accident and moved to Crewe Electric Depot, where she was ultimately scrapped in April 1997. No. 86239 is pictured in happier times at the head of a train in Platform 2 of Glasgow Central station while wearing original InterCity livery.

Class 86 Locomotive No. 86243

No. 86243 was constructed by English Electric at their Vulcan Foundry Works, Newton-le-Willows, in October 1965. She entered service shortly after, numbered E3181. She would later receive fleet number No. 86243 and carried the name *The Boys Brigade* between April 1983 and July 1993. She was withdrawn in November 2002 and is recorded as being scrapped by CF Booth, Rotherham, in October 2004. She is pictured wearing original InterCity livery at the head of a southbound train at Platform 12 at Crewe station with an unidentified Class 87 within the train formation.

Class 86 Locomotive No. 86248

Pictured wearing InterCity livery within Edinburgh Waverley station, No. 86248 was new into traffic as E3107. She was constructed at BR Doncaster Works in September 1965. Between 1981 and 2002 she carried the name *County of Clwyd/Sir Clwyd*. Like many other Class 86/2 locomotives she was withdrawn in 2002 and was placed into storage at Long Marston. In January 2009 she was prepared at Crewe Electric Depot for export to Hungary for further service. She entered service in Hungary with Floyd ZRT as 0450.001-7 in February 2009 and received a black, grey and pink livery.

Class 86 Locomotive No. 86255

New in May 1966 as E3154, she was one of the many Class 86 locomotives that were constructed by English Electric at Vulcan Foundry. By 1975 she had received flexicoil springs and was renumbered from 86042 to 86255 and regained her 100 mph maximum speed. She received the name *Penrith Beacon* in November 1980 and carried this name until she was withdrawn in 1998. She is pictured wearing full InterCity livery at the head of a southbound West Coast Main Line service passing through Lanarkshire with an InterCity-liveried Class 47 locomotive in tow. She was one of the first Class 86 locomotives to be withdrawn and still wore her InterCity livery when she was scrapped at the Immingham Railfreight terminal in 2002.

Class 86 Locomotive No. 86261

No. 86261 was constructed in September 1965 at BR Doncaster Works and entered service as E3118. She received the name *Driver John Axon GC* in February 1981 and carried this until 1992. John Axon was a driver based at Stockport who sadly died in February 1957 while attempting to stop a runaway freight train. He was posthumously awarded the George Cross for his actions. In 1992 No. 86261 received Rail Express Systems red and grey livery and she is pictured in this livery while hauling sister locomotive No. 86243 through Crewe station.

Class 86 Locomotive No. 86401

No. 86401 was constructed by English Electric in 1966 and entered service shortly after as E3199 before becoming No. 86001. After she received the flexicoil springs modification in December 1986 she became No. 86401. She received Network SouthEast livery and would remain the only Class 86 to receive this livery. She is pictured in this livery a long way from Network SouthEast territory, at Glasgow Central station. She was withdrawn in 2002 and after a few years in storage she was purchased for preservation by the AC Locomotive Group in June 2004. In 2005 she was repainted into Network SouthEast livery and in 2015 she emerged from an overhaul wearing Caledonian Sleeper livery, carrying the name *Mons Meg*. She is now used to shunt Caledonian Sleeper coaching stock to and from London Euston station.

Class 86 Locomotive No. 86416

New as E3109 in June 1965 after construction at BR Doncaster Works, she would later receive fleet number 86016 and be restricted to a maximum speed of 80 mph. In 1980 she was fitted with SAB resilient wheels, a two-part wheel separated by a rubber bearing that enabled her to return to a maximum speed of 100 mph. At this time she also received fleet number 86316. Later, in the 1980s, she received the flexicoil suspension modification that all Class 86 locomotives eventually received and became No. 86416. Withdrawal came in February 2002 and No. 86416 then spent three years in storage at Thornaby and Crewe before being scrapped in June 2005 by Booths of Rotherham.

Class 86 Locomotive No. 86419

New in September 1965 as E3120 following construction at BR Doncaster Works, she would later receive fleet number 86019 followed by 86319. By 1986 she received the flexicoil suspension modification and became No. 86419. Between 1990 and 1993 she carried the name *Post Haste 150 Years of Travelling Post Office*. The final Travelling Post Office train operated on 9 January 2004. Over the years the locomotive has worn a number of liveries including Parcels red livery as seen in this photograph, which was later changed for Rail Express Systems red and grey livery. No. 86419 was withdrawn in March 1999 and, still wearing her Rail Express Livery, was scrapped on site at Crewe in March 2003.

Class 86 Locomotive No. 86424

No. 86424 was constructed by BR at Doncaster Works in June 1965, entering service shortly after carrying fleet number E3111. She was withdrawn from traffic in 2002 and after a short period of time in storage she was sold with two other Class 86 locomotives to Network Rail for use as mobile load bank test vehicles. During her time with Network Rail she received Network Rail's all-over yellow livery. In August 2013 No. 86424 was exported to Hungary to provide spare parts for other Class 86 locomotives purchased earlier by operator Floyd ZRT. Numbered 0450.009-0 she was recorded as stored within Budapest's Keleti Depot as of May 2017.

Class 86 Locomotive No. 86611

New into traffic in September 1965 as E3171 following construction by English Electric at Vulcan Foundry, No. 86611 is pictured at Glasgow Central station at the head of a passenger service. After many years carrying Railfreight Distribution livery, as seen in this picture, she received Freightliner two-tone grey livery with the red triangle logo. This would be the last livery she carried. Sadly, No. 86611 was withdrawn after colliding with a stationary freight train at Norton Bridge on 16 October 2003. She was scrapped by the Harry Needle Railroad Company on site at Crewe Depot in February 2005.

Class 86 Locomotive No. 86621

No. 86621 was new to traffic as E3157 following construction by English Electric at Vulcan Foundry in June 1966. In 1984 she was renumbered to 86021 before becoming 86421, which was followed by 86621 in 1989. In 1995 she passed with approximately thirty other Class 86 locomotives to Freightliner, and within a few years she received the new Freightliner racing green and yellow livery. She was withdrawn from service in March 2011 after catching fire and is recorded as being scrapped at Crewe in March 2013. In happier times No. 86621 is pictured wearing Railfreight Distribution livery at Carlisle station.

Class 87 Unidentified Locomotive

In the early 1970s it was decided to extend the electrification of the West Coast Main Line (WCML) from Weaver Junction, near Crewe, to Glasgow. An order was placed for thirty-four (later increased to thirty-six) Class 87 locomotives. The Class 87 locomotives were built by BREL at Crewe Works between 1972 and 1974. Due to the gradients on the WCML between Preston and Glasgow, the Class 87 locomotives were a more powerful 5,000 hp locomotive and also had a higher top speed of 110 mph. An unidentified Class 87 locomotive is pictured undergoing overhaul at BRML Springburn Works, Glasgow.

Class 87 Unidentified Locomotive

Before beginning construction of the Class 87 locomotives, three Class 86 locomotives, Nos 86101 to 86103, were converted to become test bed locomotives for equipment that would be fitted to the new Class 87 locomotives. An unidentified Class 87 locomotive is pictured wearing original InterCity livery while heading south on the West Coast Main Line at Cleghorn level crossing.

Class 87 Locomotive No. 87006

Pictured at Liverpool Lime Street station, No. 87006 was new to service in November 1973 following construction at BREL Crewe Works. She was named *City of Glasgow* on 8 December 1977 and between 1997 and 2004 she carried the name *George Reynolds*. In 1984 she received a trial livery intended for InterCity services, which consisted of mainly grey with large BR logos and yellow cab sides. She would remain in front line service on the WCML until 2005 when she was one of three Class 87 locomotives to be acquired by freight operator DRS. Within a few years she was placed in storage at Long Marston. She was one of seventeen Class 87 locomotives to be exported to Bulgaria between 2007 and 2009, arriving after overhaul in December 2008.

Class 87 Locomotive No. 87009

Constructed by BREL at Crewe Works in November 1973, locomotive No. 87009 carried the name *City of Birmingham* between 1977 and 2003. Front line service for the Class 87 locomotives came to an end in 2005, at which point she was stored at Long Marston. After many years in storage, she was one of the last Class 87 locomotives to be exported to Bulgaria in October 2012, where she remains with Bulgarian operator Bulmarket, wearing a red and black livery and being numbered 9152 00 87 009-4.

Class 87 Locomotive No. 87013

Freshly painted into full InterCity livery complete with Swallow logos, No. 87013 is pictured approaching Crewe station just a short distance from where she was constructed in February 1974. She carried the name *John O' Gaunt* between March 1978 and December 2004. Like many Class 87 locomotives, she later returned to Crewe to be overhauled and repainted into Bulgarian Railways green and yellow livery. She was exported to Bulgaria in 2009 and can still be found in service in Bulgaria carrying fleet number No. 87013-6.

Class 87 Locomotive No. 87019

New to traffic in March 1974, locomotive No. 87019 carried the name *Sir Winston Churchill* between 1978 and 2005. In 2005 she received the name *ACoRP – The Association of Community Rail Partnership* and oddly one nameplate was green while the other was blue. She is pictured within BRML Springburn Works, Glasgow, undergoing overhaul, and would later leave the works wearing InterCity livery. Recorded as being withdrawn in June 2006, she was one of the first two Class 87 locomotives to be exported to Bulgaria in 2007, with No. 87012 being the other.

Class 87 Locomotive No. 87020

Locomotive No. 87020 is pictured at BRML Springburn Works awaiting overhaul. Between 1978 and withdrawal in 2004, she carried the name *North Briton*. No. 87020 was one of many Class 87 locomotives to be exported for further use in Bulgaria. She was overhauled and repainted into Bulgarian Railways green and yellow livery and travelled to Bulgaria in May 2009 with fellow Class 87 locomotives Nos 87029 and 87033. She was recorded as still being in active service in August 2017 and carries fleet number No. 87020–4.

Class 87 Locomotive No. 87021

No. 87021 was constructed by BREL at Crewe Works in April 1974. She carried the name *Robert the Bruce* between June 1978 and 2005. Although the majority of the Class 87 fleet was exported to Bulgaria between 2007 and 2009, No. 87021 was not one of them. After spending many years in storage at Long Marston she was scrapped by EMR Kingsbury in November 2011. No. 87021 is pictured in happier times at Edinburgh Waverley station in her original InterCity livery.

Class 87 Locomotive No. 87025

New to traffic in April 1974 following construction at BREL Crewe Works, No. 87025 is pictured at BRML Springburn Works, Glasgow. She is wearing original InterCity livery and has been prepared for the paint shop where she will receive InterCity Swallow livery. After many years in storage at Long Marston, No. 87025 was exported to Bulgaria in October 2012 and is now part of the Bulmarket fleet, where she wears a red and black livery and is still numbered No. 87025.

Class 87 Locomotive No. 87032

No. 87032 can be seen at the rear of an InterCity West Coast Main Line service in Lanarkshire. She was new to traffic in July 1974 and carried the name *Kenilworth* between 1978 and 2003. After withdrawal from service she spent many years in storage at Long Marston and was another Class 87 locomotive that was not exported to Bulgaria, being one of eleven deemed to be in poor overall condition. She is recorded as being scrapped by EMR Kingsbury in November 2010.

Class 87 Locomotive No. 87035

Constructed by BREL at Crewe Works in October 1974, locomotive No. 87035 is pictured inside Willesden Depot, London, wearing InterCity Swallow livery. This was the home depot for all the Class 87 locomotive during their active service on the West Coast Main line. No. 87035 was named *Robert Burns* in April 1978 and still carries the name today. Happily, she is one of three Class 87 locomotives to be preserved in the UK and is currently a resident at the Crewe Heritage Centre, just a short distance from where she was constructed. Upon entering preservation she first carried BR blue livery but she has now been repainted into original InterCity livery.

Class 87 Locomotive No. 87101

The last Class 87 locomotive to be constructed was No. 87036, although she never carried this number in service. She became a test bed locomotive for new electrical equipment that would be used in the Class 90 locomotives and remained on test until 1976 when she finally entered service as locomotive No. 87101. Upon sectorisation No. 87101 passed to Railfreight Distribution and she became the only Class 87 to receive Railfreight Distribution livery. Upon withdrawal from service in January 1998 she was sold to Alstom for spare parts and is recorded as being scrapped by HNRC at Barrow Hill in 2002. She is pictured attending an open day event at Crewe Depot on 3 May 1997, and at this time carries BR blue livery.

Class 89 Locomotive No. 89001

Locomotive No. 89001 was constructed in 1986 as a production prototype by BREL at Crewe Works as a sub-contractor to Brush Engineering. The locomotive was designed as a multi-purpose AC electric locomotive that was capable of speeds up to 125 mph and could, therefore, be used for both passenger services on the East and West Coast Main Lines as well as freight services. After testing she entered service on the East Coast Main Line in 1987, being based at Bounds Green Depot, London, where this picture of No. 89001 in InterCity Swallow livery was taken.

Class 90 Locomotive No. 90006

The next class of AC electric locomotives to be built were the Class 90s. A total of fifty were ordered with construction taking place at BREL Crewe Works between 1987 and 1990. Locomotive No. 90006 was new to traffic in September 1988 and is pictured wearing InterCity Swallow livery at the rear of a WCML service that has just arrived into London Euston station. In March 1997 Virgin Trains became the new operator of the West Coast Main Line franchise, and shortly after Nos 90001 to 90015 received the new Virgin Trains livery. In 2004 she passed with the rest of the Virgin Trains Class 90 locomotive fleet to the Great Eastern Main Line, where she remains in service today.

Class 90 Locomotive No. 90009

New to traffic in September 1988 following construction at BREL Crewe Works, locomotive No. 90009 is pictured undergoing overhaul at BRML, Springburn Works, Glasgow. She is wearing InterCity Swallow livery and the Class 90 locomotives were the first class of locomotives to carry this livery. She would later receive Virgin Trains livery before moving to Greater Anglia in 2004 and now carries Abellio Greater Anglia livery.

Class 90 Locomotive No. 90010

No. 90010 was constructed in October 1988 at BREL Crewe Works and has been named twice so far. Between November 1989 and July 2004 she carried the name *275 Railway Squadron (Volunteers)* later between June 2011 and July 2014 she was named *Bressingham Steam & Gardens*. She remains in service as part of the Abellio Greater Anglia fleet, which is based at Norwich Crown Point Depot.

Class 90 Locomotive No. 90015

No. 90015 was constructed at BREL Crewe Works in November 1988. Between 1989 and 1997 she was named *BBC North West* followed by *The International Brigades Spain 1936–1939* between 1998 and 2004. In 2008 she received the name *Colchester Castle*. She is pictured wearing InterCity Swallow livery on 26 April 1992 at Manchester Longsight Depot during an open day event.

Class 90 Locomotive No. 90017

No. 90017 is pictured wearing InterCity Swallow livery at Carlisle station. She was constructed at BREL Crewe Works in December 1988 and with the sectorisation of British Rail she was one of five locomotives numbered 90016 to 90020 to pass to the Parcels sector. Within five years of this picture being taken she had received Rail Express Systems red and grey livery.

Class 90 Locomotive No. 90017

A later view of No. 90017, this time taken at Crewe station. By the time this photograph was taken she had been repainted into Rail Express Systems livery and would later receive the name *Rail Express Systems Quality Assured*. She was placed into storage at Crewe in November 2006 with an electrical fault and it is unclear if she will return to traffic in the future.

Class 90 Locomotive No. 90018

No. 90018 was constructed by BREL at Crewe Works in December 1988. She entered service wearing InterCity Swallow livery but upon sectorisation she passed to the Parcels sector. She is pictured with sister Class 90 locomotive No. 90019 passing Manchester Longsight Depot. No. 90018 would later pass to EWS Railways and receive EWS maroon and yellow livery. In January 2013 she was outshopped in DB Schenker cherry red livery and was still in active service with the company in 2017. She received the name *Pride of Bellshill* in December 2015.

Class 90 Locomotive No. 90021

New in January 1989 following construction at BREL Crewe Works, No. 90021 is pictured at Edinburgh Waverley station, having been freshly painted into Railfreight Distribution livery. Under sectorisation locomotives Nos 90021 to 90024 were allocated to Railfreight Distribution, where they retained their maximum speed of 110 mph to enable them to assist passenger trains if required. Between February 2001 and June 2002 she was renumbered 90221 and operated passenger services over the East Coast Main Line. Since 2015 she has been in storage at Crewe, where she is awaiting maintenance.

Class 90 Locomotive No. 90025

The final Class 90 locomotive to be delivered in InterCity Swallow livery was No. 90025. She was constructed at BREL Crewe Works in March 1989. By June 1992 she had been repainted into Railfreight Distribution livery and it would be this livery she would carry until she was withdrawn from service. She has been in storage at Crewe since 2004 and after thirteen years in open storage is now in a very poor condition, but she is still wearing her Railfreight Distribution livery.

Class 90 Locomotive No. 90035

The next eleven Class 90 locomotives, numbered No. 90026 to No. 90036, were delivered in Mainline livery. In 1991 the Class 90 locomotives numbered 90026 to 90050 were all renumbered, becoming No. 90126 to No. 90150. They had their ETH isolated and a revised top speed of 75 mph imposed. At the same time they were allocated to the Railfreight Distribution sector and began to receive Railfreight Distribution livery. No. 90035 is pictured at Glasgow Central station during her time numbered No. 90035 while carrying Mainline livery.

Class 90 Locomotive No. 90036

The final Class 90 locomotive to be delivered in Mainline livery was No. 90036, which entered service after construction in April 1990. By 1993 she had lost her Mainline livery and had received a revised Railfreight Distribution livery with additional yellow wrapping around the cab sides and on the roof. This was known as Sybic livery. In 2013 she received DB Schenker's cherry red livery and more recently her DB Schenker fleet name was changed to DB Cargo. In 2017, No. 90036 is still an active member of the DB Cargo fleet.

Class 90 Locomotive No. 90037

Class 90 locomotives numbered from 90037 to 90050 were all delivered wearing Railfreight livery complete with Distribution subsector markings. No. 90037 is pictured at Glasgow Central station at the head of a passenger service. This photograph was taken very soon after she entered service in April 1990. I remember this day well as I was due to travel on this service and was not expecting a shiny new Railfreight Distribution-liveried Class 90 locomotive to be hauling the train. Remarkably, she carried this livery until May 2001, when she received EWS livery. She was named *Spirit of Dagenham* in May 2001 and carried a traditional Ford badge above her nameplates.

Class 90 Locomotive No. 90042

Another nearly new Class 90 locomotive, No. 90042, wearing Railfreight Distribution livery, is pictured at London Euston station. During this period of time many nearly new Railfreight Distribution Class 90 locomotives were used for main line passenger work. No. 90042 was constructed by BREL at Crewe Works in May 1990.

Class 90 Locomotive No. 90042

A later photograph of No. 90042, this time taken at Edinburgh Waverley station. She was one of eleven Class 90 locomotives to pass to Freightliner during BR privatisation. She would go on to receive two-tone grey livery with the Freightliner red triangle logo and in 2014 she received the current Freightliner green and yellow Powerhaul livery.

Class 90 Locomotive No. 90044

No. 90044 entered service shortly after construction at BREL Crewe Works in June 1990. She is pictured wearing Railfreight Distribution livery at the head of a West Coast Main Line service at Glasgow Central station. Looking closely at the photograph, the pantograph and the buffer beam look almost new, and so it is likely that this photograph was taken not long after the locomotive entered service. Between July 1991 and September 2002 she was renumbered No. 90144. Locomotive No. 90044 would carry Railfreight Distribution livery until at least 1995.

Class 90 Locomotive No. 90046

Class 90, locomotive No. 90046 is pictured arriving into Edinburgh Waverley station. The train would have been a charter train and the leading coach is a First Class Mk 1 vehicle in InterCity livery. Locomotive No. 90046 was constructed at BREL Crewe Works in June 1990. She carried Railfreight Distribution livery from new and was one of eleven locomotives, numbers 90016 and 90041–90050, to pass to Freightliner as part of the British Rail privatisation. She currently wears Freightliner 'Racing Green' livery.

Class 90 Locomotive No. 90050

The final Class 90 locomotive to be constructed was locomotive No. 90050. She was under construction when this photograph was taken at BREL Crewe Works during an open day event on 21 July 1990. She would later enter service in November 1990, being allocated to the Railfreight sector. Sadly, her operational life was cut short when she caught fire in September 2004. By December 2004 she had been withdrawn and was stored at Crewe. She is currently still stored in a semi-stripped condition at Crewe Basford Hall Yard.

Class 90 Locomotive No. 90050

A later view of locomotive No. 90050 at Carlisle station. She did not carry the fleet number 90050 for long, being renumbered No. 90150 in July 1991. She was later renumbered back to 90050 in August 2002. She would pass to Freightliner as part of the British Rail privatisation and shortly afterwards received Freightliner's two-tone grey livery with red triangle logos. It was this livery she carried when she caught fire in September 2004 and was subsequently withdrawn.

Class 90 Locomotive No. 90128

In September 1992 three Class 90 locomotives received Continental railway liveries in connection with the Freight Connection event that took place that year at the NEC Birmingham. Locomotive No. 90128 received the blue and yellow livery of the Belgian state rail operator SNCB. She also received the name *Vrachtverbinding*. Although this livery was applied to mark the 1992 event, remarkably the locomotive was kept in this livery until July 2003. In 2017 she remains in traffic with DB Cargo while still wearing her EWS livery. No. 90128 is pictured at Crewe Depot where she took part in an open day event on 3 May 1997.

Class 90 Locomotive No. 90129

The second Class 90 to receive a Continental livery in September 1992 was locomotive No. 90129. This locomotive received a predominantly red livery for German state operator DB, which she would carry until 2003, when she received EWS Railways maroon and yellow livery. Interestingly, this would not be the last time this particular locomotive would carry DB livery. After EWS Railways was acquired by DB in 2009, No. 90129, now renumbered back to 90029, was outshopped in December 2012 and then wore DB Schenker red livery. Pictured shortly after receiving DB livery in 1992, locomotive No. 90129 pauses on Platform 4 at Carlisle station for a crew changeover.

Class 90 Locomotive No. 90130

No. 90130 was the final Class 90 to receive a Continental livery in September 1992. This particular locomotive received French rail operator SNCF's two-tone grey and orange livery. No. 90130 entered service as No. 90030 shortly after construction at BREL Crewe Works in May 1989. Over the years she has carried two names. Between September 1992 and June 1999 she was named *Fretconnection* and later during an open day event at Crewe, on 21 May 2000, she received the name *Crewe Locomotive Works,* being named after the works where she was constructed eleven years prior. Sadly, she has been in storage since 2006, and after more than ten years it is unclear if she will return to active service.

Class 90 Locomotive No. 90131

Locomotive No. 90131 was constructed by BREL at their Crewe Works in September 1989 and entered service as locomotive No. 90031. She carried the number 90131 between July 1991 and June 1999 before reverting to 90031. She is pictured wearing Mainline livery while awaiting her next duty. This locomotive has been in long-term storage with wheelset problems since December 2007.

Class 91 Locomotive No. 91002

In 1985 GEC won the tender to construct thirty-one Class 91 locomotives for operation on the newly electrified East Coast Main Line. The Class 91 locomotives were powerful 6,000 hp locomotives capable of a top speed of 140 mph. They became known as InterCity 225 trains, the 225 referring to their top speed in km/h. No. 91002 is pictured in InterCity Swallow livery at the rear of a Glasgow Central to London Kings Cross service near Cleghorn level crossing on the West Coast Main Line. The author's car, a Citroen BX that was new in 1990, can be seen in the background of this photograph.

Class 91 Locomotive No. 91002

No. 91002 was constructed by BREL at Crewe Works in April 1988. She was delivered in InterCity Swallow livery and after the privatisation of British Rail she received GNER blue with red stripe livery. No. 91002 is pictured at Doncaster station outside Doncaster Works and is wearing InterCity Swallow livery. Note that she is missing her lower valance from under the buffer beam.

Class 91 Locomotive No. 91005

The Class 91 locomotives had their traction motors fitted within the body of the locomotive which was then connected via cardan shafts to bogie mounted gearboxes. They also had their main transformers mounted under solebar level. No. 91005 was constructed by BREL at their Crewe Works in May 1988. She is pictured wearing InterCity Swallow livery at her home depot, Bounds Green, London, in the company of other Class 91 locomotives.

Class 91 Unidentified Locomotive

Part of the design specification for the Class 91 locomotives was for them to be able to operate as a conventional locomotive when needed and haul other classes and types of train. For that reason the Class 91 locomotives featured an asymmetrical design, with a streamlined cab at one end and a conventional cab at the other. Class 91 locomotives very rarely operate 'blunt end' first, but when they do they are restricted to a maximum speed of 110 mph. An unidentified Class 91 locomotive is pictured in a bay platform at Doncaster station and is wearing InterCity Swallow livery.

Class 91 Locomotive No. 91010

Although the Class 91 locomotives were designed with a maximum speed of 140 mph, they have only ever operated at 125 mph. No. 91010 set a new British Railways speed record for a locomotive on 17 September 1989, achieving a speed of 161.7 mph near Stoke Bank and now carries a plaque commemorating this event. She is pictured at London Kings Cross station while getting ready to depart with a northbound service. No. 91010 was new in April 1989 after construction by BREL at Crewe Works.

Class 91 Locomotive No. 91013

Locomotive No. 91013 was constructed at Crewe Works in April 1990. She was renumbered to 91113 following overhaul in May 2002. Over the years the East Coast Main Line franchise has changed hands and as a result she has worn many liveries; currently, she carries Virgin East Coast Trains livery. No. 91013 is pictured at the north end of an InterCity 225 train upon arrival at York station and is wearing the InterCity Swallow livery she received when new.

Class 91 Locomotive No. 91015

No. 91015 was constructed by BREL at Crewe Works in May 1990. She is pictured at her home depot, Bounds Green, London, and is wearing the InterCity Swallow livery that she carried when new. After overhaul in August 2002 she became No. 91115.

Class 91 Locomotive No. 91017

In another 'blunt end' view of a Class 91 locomotive, No. 91017 is pictured at Bounds Green Depot, London. No. 91017 was constructed at BREL Crewe Works in July 1990 and after overhaul in February 2002 she became No. 91117. She currently carries Virgin East Coast Trains livery.

Class 91 Locomotive No. 91017

The Class 91 locomotives have always been allocated to Bounds Green Depot, London, which is the location of this photograph. Three Class 91 locomotives can be seen, Nos 91017, 91005 and 91015, and all are wearing InterCity Swallow livery. The unique Class 89 locomotive *Avocet* can also be seen next to the Class 91 locomotives.

Class 91 Locomotive No. 91018

Pictured upon arrival at Leeds station, No. 91018 is seen in InterCity Swallow livery. When new the Class 91 locomotives featured a Silver Swallow badge on the front grill, as can be seen in this photograph. No. 91018 was new into service in August 1990. She was renumbered 91118 in November 2002 following overhaul and is currently painted in Virgin East Coast Trains livery.

Class 91 Locomotives No. 91025 and No. 91029

Two Class 91 locomotives, Nos 91025 and 91029, are pictured at London Kings Cross station. No. 91025 was constructed in October 1990 while No. 91029 was built in January 1991. No. 91025 became No. 91125 after overhaul in January 2003, with No. 91029 becoming No. 91129 in October 2002. Both locomotives now carry Virgin East Coast Trains livery.

Class 91 Locomotive No. 91030

No. 91030, the penultimate Class 91 locomotive, is pictured departing from Edinburgh Waverley station while wearing InterCity Swallow livery. She was new in March 1991 following construction at BREL Crewe Works. On 26 September 1991, sister locomotive No. 91031 completed the journey between London Kings Cross and Edinburgh Waverley in a record time of three hours, twenty-nine minutes and thirty seconds.

Class 92 Locomotive No. 92020

The next class of AC electric locomotives to be ordered were the Class 92 locomotives. Forty-six were constructed by Brush at Loughborough between 1993 and 1996. They are powerful 6,700 hp locomotives that were designed to be used for international freight services. They were also intended to be used for 'Nightstar' international sleeper services before the project was cancelled. In 2000, Eurostar, the current owner of No. 92020, offered her for sale, along with six other examples they owned. A buyer could not be found and the locomotives entered long-term storage at Crewe.

AJ41 (RBR) Restaurant Buffet Mk 1 Vehicle No. 1691

Mk 1 Restaurant Buffet vehicle No. 1691 was constructed by Pressed Steel in 1961. No. 1691 is pictured freshly painted in InterCity livery outside BRML Springburn Works. A few years after this photograph was taken, No. 1691 became part of the Venice Simplon-Orient-Express. Remarkably, she is one of a very few Mk 1 vehicles that can still be found in active service in 2017, now being part of the Riviera Trains fleet.

AA21 (SK) Corridor Second Mk 1 Unidentified Vehicle

A Mk 1 Corridor Second vehicle is pictured at London Paddington station. She is wearing Pilkington K Glass livery and was one of a number of Mk 1 coaches based at Steamtown Railway Centre, Carnforth, that wore this promotional livery around this time. Mk 1 coaches were constructed between 1951 and 1963, with the final Mk 1 coaches being withdrawn from regular main line use in 2005.

AX51 Generator Van Mk 1 Vehicle No. 6311

Vehicle No. 6311 was constructed by Pressed Steel in 1958. She is pictured at Edinburgh Waverley station while wearing InterCity livery. Over the years she has also carried fleet numbers 80903, 92011 and 92911. When this photograph was taken, in around 1992, she had recently been converted from a standard Gangwayed Brake Van into a Generator Van with the intention of using her to provide power to coaches on trains hauled by Class 37 locomotives within Scotland – including sleeper train services.

NS (POS) Post Office Sorting Van Mk 1 Vehicle No. 80357

Vehicle No. 80357 is pictured at Doncaster Works during an open day event. She had recently been outshopped in Royal Mail livery when the photograph was taken. History records that the first train to operate with mail being sorted on board was in 1838. Sadly, Royal Mail terminated the contract for the Travelling Post Office in 2003 and the last train ran on 9 January 2004.

NCX Newspaper Van Mk 1 Unidentified Vehicle

An unidentified Mk 1 vehicle, believed to be a NCX Newspaper Van, is pictured at Carlisle station while wearing Rail Express Systems red and grey livery. She would have begun life as a Gangwayed Brake Van before becoming an NCX Newspaper Van. Many Mk 1 Gangwayed Brake Vans (BG) received new B4 bogies in place of the original B1 bogies to make them suitable for a maximum speed of 100 mph. This vehicle has Commonwealth bogies, which were fitted to later Mk 1 vehicles from new.

NDX Gangwayed Brake Van Mk 1 Vehicle No. 84420

Constructed by Pressed Steel in 1957, Mk 1 NDX Gangwayed Brake Van No. 84420 is pictured outside BRML Springburn Works, looking smart in Parcels red livery. The coach next to her is a Mk 2 design and the differences in the body profiles can be seen clearly in this photograph. The Mk 1 design featured a separate steel underframe, which supported the steel-panelled, unstressed body.

NOX General Utility Van Mk 1 Vehicle No. 95105

Vehicle No. 95105 was a General Utility Van suitable for 100 mph running. As can be seen in this photograph she was wired for ETH and has Commonwealth bogies. She previously carried number 93126 and was constructed by Pressed Steel in 1958. Vehicle No. 95105 is pictured at an open day event while wearing Rail Express Systems red and grey livery.

Observation Lounge Car Vehicle No. 99965

Observation Lounge Car No. 99965 is pictured at Inverness station. She was one of forty-four coaches constructed by Metropolitan Cammell in 1960 for services on the East Coast Main Line. Originally known as a Pullman Car she carried the number E319 before receiving Vehicle No. 99965. She is wearing Royal Scotsman livery and still carries this livery in 2017, regularly forming part of the Royal Scotsman train. She can often still be seen at Inverness station as part of her Royal Scotsman duties.

Gresley Trailer Kitchen 99960

Gresley Trailer Kitchen Car 99960 is pictured at Inverness station and was at this time part of the Royal Scotsman train. She was constructed by Birmingham Railway Carriage & Wagon Company in 1935 and is of teak wood construction. She entered service with LNER, numbered 23890, and is recorded as being withdrawn in 1961. She entered preservation in 1989 and currently resides on the North Yorkshire Moors Railway at Pickering, where she is currently undergoing long-term restoration.

Pullman Parlour First Vehicle No. 99963

Vehicle No. 99963 was one of forty-four vehicles constructed by Metropolitan Cammell in 1960 and was a Pullman Parlour First vehicle. She was originally numbered E331 and carried the name *Topaz* from new. For many years she operated Pullman services on the East Coast Main Line and, following the withdrawal of Pullman services over this route in 1978, vehicle No. E331 was placed into storage. In 1989 she was rebuilt as a sleeper carriage and featured four twin cabins. She is pictured wearing Royal Scotsman livery at Inverness station.

GS5 (HSBV) HST Barrier Vehicle Mk 2A Vehicle No. 6346

British Rail converted a selection of coaches of both Mk 1 and Mk 2 designs to become barrier vehicles. These barrier vehicles were used to permit a non-HST locomotive to haul Class 43 HST power cars and or Mk 3 HST coaching stock vehicles. Vehicle No. 6346 began life in 1967 as Vehicle No. 9422 and was constructed by BR Derby Works as a Mk 2A Open Brake Second vehicle. She is pictured wearing InterCity livery attached to a Class 43 power car at Leeds station. Later in life she would receive blue GNER livery.

AC2Z (TSO) Open Standard Mk 2 Vehicle 5212

Over 1,870 Mk 2 vehicles were constructed between 1963 and 1974 and all were constructed at BR Derby Works. The design of the Mk 2 coach evolved over the years and Mk 2 coaches can be one of seven different variants, ranging from Mk 2 and Mk 2A through to Mk 2F. Vehicle No. 5212 was a Mk 2 Open Standard coach (TSO) that was constructed in 1966. She is pictured at BRML Springburn Works carrying LNER tourist green and cream livery and the name *Capercailzie*. She would see extensive use on the Inverness to Kyle of Lochalsh line and often worked trains formed with a former Class 101 DMU observation carriage.

AD1E (FO) Open First Mk 2E Vehicle No. 3245

Vehicle No. 3245 was a Mk 2E Open First coach that was constructed at BR Derby Works in 1973 and is pictured in the yard at BRML Springburn Works on a wintry day. She carries Scotrail livery, which was similar to InterCity livery but had a blue stripe in place of the InterCity red stripe.

AD1E (FO) Open First Mk 2E Unidentified Vehicle

The Mk 2E vehicles had smaller toilets and had luggage racks fitted opposite the toilets at each end of the coach. They were the first variant of the Mk 2 design not to specify any compartment type vehicles. An unidentified Mk 2E Open First vehicle is pictured inside BRML Springburn Works paint shop while receiving InterCity livery.

AE2E (BSO) Open Brake Standard Vehicle No. 9500

Vehicle No. 9500 was a Mk 2E Open Brake Standard coach that was constructed in 1972 at BR Derby Works. She featured thirty-two seats, one toilet and a brake van compartment. She is pictured at BRML Springburn works while receiving a fresh application of InterCity livery.

AC2F (TSO) Open Standard Mk 2F Unidentified Vehicle

Over 470 Mk 2F coaches were built between 1973 and 1975 at BR Derby Works. The Mk 2F was the final variety of the Mk 2 coach and, like the Mk 2E vehicles, no compartment type vehicles were constructed. An unidentified Mk 2F vehicle is pictured at BMRL Springburn Works in InterCity livery. The logotype used for the InterCity name was changed after 1987 from the style seen in this picture to serif upper case letters in an italic font.

Class 488/2 Victoria–Gatwick Trailer Set Mk 2F Vehicle 72508

Vehicle No. 72508 was constructed by BR Derby Works in 1974 as a Mk 2F vehicle and was originally numbered 3409. She was one of seventy-seven Mk 2F coaches that were converted between 1983 and 1984 to become unpowered trailer sets for operation on Gatwick Express services. They were designed to operate with a Class 73 locomotive at one end of the train and a Class 489 GLV driving vehicle at the other end. Class 488/2 No. 8209 is pictured in InterCity livery with Gatwick Express logos at Stewarts Lane Depot, London. Upon withdrawal from service in 2004 she spent four years in storage before being sold to Mainline Steam Trust, New Zealand, where she remains, also in storage.

Class 489 Victoria–Gatwick GLV DMBSO Vehicle No. 68503

Vehicle No. 68503 was constructed by BR at Eastleigh in 1959. She was originally numbered 61277 and was part of a Class 414 2HAP unit. She was one of ten vehicles converted by Eastleigh Works in 1984 to become GLV vehicles for operation of Gatwick Express services. She could normally be found at the London end of the train with a Class 73 locomotive at the other end. The train would operate in push-pull mode, but unlike other push-pull services both the locomotive and GLV vehicle provided power. Class 489 No. 9104 is pictured at Stewarts Lane Depot, London, while wearing original InterCity livery. Upon withdrawal in 2004 she was one of four Class 489 GLV vehicles to be preserved and currently resides at the Spa Valley Railway.

AF2F (DBSO) Driving Open Brake Standard Mk 2F Vehicle No. 9701

In 1979 ten Mk 2F Open Brake Standard vehicles were converted at BRML Springburn to become Driving Open Brake Standard vehicles, known as DBSO vehicles. The conversion work involved fitting a driving cab into the brake van end of the vehicle and fitting them with TDM equipment to enable them to work in push-pull mode with Class 47/7 locomotives. They were initially used on Scotrail Glasgow to Edinburgh services. Vehicle No. 9701 was constructed by BR Derby Works in 1974 and was originally numbered 9528. She is pictured at London Liverpool Street station following her transfer south from Scotland to operate services between London and Norwich. At the time this photograph was taken she had been rebuilt with a full-width cab following the removal of the end gangway.

AF2F (DBSO) Driving Open Brake Standard Mk 2F Vehicle No. 9704

Vehicle No. 9704 was constructed by BR Derby Works in 1974. She was a Mk 2F Open Brake Standard vehicle and entered service carrying fleet number 9512 before being converted into a Driving Open Brake Standard vehicle (DBSO) in 1979. In 1990, following the arrival of Class 158 units, the DBSO vehicles were transferred from Scotland to Norwich Crown Point Depot and operated on services between London and Norwich. By 2006, by which time they were over thirty years old, the DBSO vehicles were finally withdrawn from front line services. Vehicle No. 9704 is pictured in Scotrail livery at Glasgow Queen Street station. At the time this photograph was taken she featured a half cab and retained her end gangway.

AU4G (SLEP) Sleeping Car with Pantry Mk 3A Vehicle No. 10543

A total of 848 Mk 3 coaching stock vehicles were built between 1975 and 1988 by BR Derby Works, including 208 sleeping carriages. When built there were two variants of Mk 3 sleeper coaches. Eighty-eight vehicles were designated ASAG (SLE) sleeping cars, comprising thirteen compartments, while the other 120 vehicles, including No. 10543, were known as AU4G (SLEP) sleeping cars, which comprised a pantry and twelve sleeping compartments. Although the sleeper carriages were based on Mk 3A vehicles, unlike Mk 3A vehicles the sleeper carriages featured controlled emission toilets and had built-in illuminated tail lamps. Vehicle No. 10543 was built in 1981 and is pictured outside BRML Springburn Works in BR blue and grey livery.

GH2G (TS) Trailer Standard Mk 3 Vehicle No. 42320

Vehicle No. 42320 was constructed at BR Derby Works in 1982 as a HST Trailer Standard vehicle. Although similar in appearance and construction to a Mk 3A non-HST vehicle, the two types of vehicle are not compatible with each other due to operating with different on-board power supplies. Vehicle No. 42320 is pictured in BR blue and grey livery and carries InterCity 125 lettering. She would later receive InterCity livery, which was followed by Virgin Trains livery. No. 42320 was one of a small number of HST Trailer Standard vehicles to be converted in 2009 to Trailer Standard Micro Buffet vehicles (TSMB), being designated 2N2G.

GK2G (TRSB) Trailer Buffet Standard Mk 3 Unidentified Vehicle

The Mk 3 vehicles featured new BT10 bogies with coil springs, hydraulic dampers and air suspension between the bogies and the coach body. This gave a superior level of comfort compared to a Mk 2 coach. They were also fitted with disc brakes and had a maximum speed of 125 mph. An unidentified Trailer Buffet Standard vehicle (TRSB) is pictured in InterCity livery as part of a HST formation. The red stripe above the windows denotes the buffet area of the coach. Many buffet and kitchen vehicles were later converted into Standard Class Trailer vehicles.

NZ (DLV) Driving Brake Van Mk 3 DVT Vehicle No. 82133

A total of fifty-two Mk 3 DVT vehicles were constructed by BR Derby Works in 1988. They entered service shortly after on West Coast Main Line services and could normally be found at the London end of trains. They were built to work in push-pull mode with Class 86, Class 87 and Class 90 locomotives. DVT No. 82133 is pictured wearing InterCity Swallow livery and during her time on the West Coast Main Line she would later receive Virgin Trains livery. Many of the Mk 3 DVT vehicles, including No. 82133, were later transferred to Great Eastern Main Line services, which permitted the earlier Mk 2F DBSO vehicles to be withdrawn.

NZ (DLV) Driving Brake Van Mk 3 DVT Vehicle No. 82141

While the Mk 2F DBSO vehicles were fitted with passenger accommodation, the DVT vehicles were not permitted to carry passengers, due to operating at speeds in excess of 100 mph. They were, however, fitted with a guard's compartment and were able to be used as storage vans. Many Mk 3 DVT vehicles became surplus to requirements after the introduction of new Pendolino trains to West Coast Main Line services in 2002 and were consequently placed into storage. Vehicle No. 82141 was constructed at BR Derby Works in 1988 and is pictured on a very wet day at Glasgow Central station not long after entering service. DVT No. 82141 would later receive Virgin Trains livery and is currently stored at Long Marston.

AJ1J (RFM) Restaurant Buffet First (Modular) Mk 4 Vehicle No. 10312

The next coaching stock to be ordered by BR was the Mk 4 vehicle. A total of 314 vehicles were ordered and were delivered between 1989 and 1992 for services on the newly electrified East Coast Main Line. The vehicles were constructed by Metro Cammell and GEC Alstom at the Washwood Heath factory near Birmingham. Restaurant Buffet First vehicle No. 10312 was constructed in 1989 and is pictured at Kings Cross station, London, in InterCity livery. Thanks to Project Mallard, the Mk 4 rolling stock received an extensive refurbishment between 2003 and 2005. As part of this refurbishment the Restaurant Buffet First vehicles were turned round in the train formation and were converted to Restaurant Buffet Standard vehicles. This was to increase the Standard allocation on each train set.

AD1J (FO) Open First Mk 4 Unidentified Vehicle

The Mk 4 coaches were designed with a body profile that would permit tilting equipment to be retrofitted, allowing a tilt of six degrees. They were also fitted with sliding plug doors, controlled emission toilets and fully enclosed gangways. The Mk 4 vehicles are capable of speeds up to 140 mph, but have only ever operated at a maximum speed of 125 mph. An unidentified Mk 4 Open First vehicle is pictured in InterCity livery at London Kings Cross station not long after entering service.

NZ (DLV) Driving Brake Van Mk 4 DVT Vehicle No. 82207

With the introduction of Mk 4 coaches on to the East Coast Main Line, services were operated in push-pull mode. Trains would be formed with a Class 91 locomotive, which was normally to be found at the north end of the train, and a Mk 4 Driving Van Trailer (DVT) at the rear. The Mk 4 DVT vehicles were similar to the Mk 3 DVT vehicles that operated on West Coast Main Line services but were capable of 140 mph. DVT vehicle No. 82207 is pictured at London Kings Cross station and is wearing InterCity livery.

NZ (DLV) Driving Brake Van Mk 4 DVT Unidentified Vehicle

An unidentified Mk 4 DVT vehicle is pictured at Leeds station. Like the Mk 3 DVT vehicles, passengers are not carried in the DVT vehicle due to operating at speeds in excess of 100 mph. They are, however, fitted with a guard's compartment and can be used for the storage of bikes and luggage.

NZ (DLV) Driving Brake Van Mk 4 DVT Vehicle No. 82223

DVT Vehicle No. 82223 is pictured under construction at BREL Crewe Works during an open day event on 21 July 1990 and, as can be seen, she is resting on temporary bogies. Of the thirty-one Mk 4 DVT vehicles constructed, only one has been scrapped. This was vehicle No. 82221, which was involved in the Great Heck accident in February 2001.

Class 370 Advanced Passenger Train APT No. 370 003

The Advanced Passenger Train (APT) project was intended to transform services on the West Coast Main Line. Three service prototypes were constructed but they only operated for a month in December 1981 before being withdrawn due to many teething problems. They returned to service in 1984 and continued to operate until the winter of 1985, at which point they were withdrawn again. By this stage the diesel-powered High Speed Train (HST) was proving to be a much greater success. The APT set a new speed record of 162.2 mph in December 1979. After being withdrawn from service in 1985, the APT vehicles were placed into storage until 1987, when two of the three sets were scrapped. The final set, numbered 370 003, was preserved and can be found at Crewe Heritage Centre, where this photograph was taken.

Class 205 Unit No. 205 029 Vehicle No. 60817

The Class 205 units were diesel electric multiple units, known as DEMUs, which were powered by an above-floor 600 hp diesel engine. They were used by the Southern Region for services over non-electrified routes. They were constructed at BR Eastleigh Works between 1957 and 1962 and, remarkably, some Class 205 units remained in service until 2004, when they were replaced with Class 171 Turbostar units. Class 205 No. 205 029 is pictured attending an open day event at Eastleigh Depot on 27 September 1992. Sadly, she was one of the units involved in the Cowden rail crash on 15 October 1994 and was scrapped shortly after.

Class 205 Unit No. 205 031 Vehicle No. 60149

Unit No. 205 031 was constructed at BR Eastleigh Works in 1962 and entered service shortly after, being numbered 1131. She is pictured at Salisbury station and is wearing BR blue and grey livery. This would be the livery she would carry until she was withdrawn in July 1993, at which point she was then converted to become a Sandite unit and was numbered 930301. She later received Railtrack livery and currently remains in storage at St Leonards Depot. The black triangle painted on the front of the unit denotes that this driving vehicle contains the engine and brake van compartment.

Class 302 Unit No. 302 991 Vehicle No. 68208

The Class 302 units were constructed at BR York Works between 1958 and 1960. They were originally designated AM2 units and a total of 112 sets were constructed. They were based on Mk 1 coaches and featured slam doors. All Class 302 units were refurbished between 1981 and 1982 with many remaining in service until 1999, by which time they were forty years old. In 1988 a number of Class 302 units were renumbered to become Class 302/9 units. They all became three-coach units with four units becoming Parcel units and three becoming departmental Sandite units. Unit No. 302 991 is pictured inside Ilford Depot and has been repainted into Royal Mail red and yellow livery. As part of her conversion to a Parcel unit she has been fitted with roller shutter doors.

Class 302 Unit No. 302 996 Vehicle No. ADB 977600

Three Class 302 units were converted to become departmental Sandite units for the East Anglia region. Vehicle No. ADB 977600 was originally numbered 75061 and was constructed at BR York Works in 1958. Unit No. 302 996 is pictured in the yard at Ilford Depot and is wearing an attractive green, cream and blue livery. She would later be renumbered to become unit 937 996, although she continued to carry 302 996. She is recorded as being withdrawn and scrapped in 1996.

Class 302 Unit No. 302 998 Vehicle No. ADB977606

The final Class 302 Sandite unit was numbered 302 998. She became a Sandite unit in 1988 and is pictured wearing Network SouthEast livery at Ilford Depot. Unit No. 302 998 was later renumbered to 937 998, although she continued to carry number 302 998. She would later receive Railtrack livery and is recorded as being withdrawn in 1998 and scrapped in 1999.

Class 303 Unit No. 303 014 Vehicle No. 75579

The Class 303 units were constructed by Pressed Steel, Linwood, between 1959 and 1961. They were originally designated AM3 units before later becoming Class 303 units. Following introduction to service the Class 303 units were quickly referred to as Blue Trains, owning to their striking Caledonian Blue livery. Unit No. 303 014 is pictured shortly after joining the West Coast Main Line near Cleghorn level crossing. She is operating a service from Lanark to Milngavie and is wearing Strathclyde PTE livery, which was introduced in the 1980s.

Class 303 Unit No. 303 048 Vehicle No. 75808

Following the introduction of new Class 320 units in 1989, a number of Class 303 units were declared surplus. Twelve un-refurbished Class 303 units were transferred to Manchester Longsight Depot. They were all withdrawn around 1993 apart from unit No. 303 048, which had returned to Glasgow in 1990. She was the sole remaining un-refurbished Class 303 unit and, shortly after returning to Scotland, was repainted into original Blue Train livery. Unit No. 303 048 is pictured approaching Paisley Gilmour Street station in 1991. She was operating a number of services between Glasgow Central and Greenock to celebrate the 150th anniversary of the Glasgow, Paisley & Greenock Railway. It was originally intended to preserve No. 303 048 but, being un-refurbished, this meant that she still contained harmful asbestos and as a result she was later scrapped.

Class 303 Unit No. 303 052 Vehicle No. 75762

Unit No. 303 052 is pictured at MC Metals, Springburn, Glasgow. Although she has received Strathclyde PTE livery she has not been refurbished and is awaiting scrapping. In the background can be seen a Class 311 unit, No. 311 099. The Class 311 units were very similar to the Class 303 units and nineteen were constructed in 1967 by Cravens of Sheffield.

Class 303 Unit No. 303 069 Vehicle No. 75607

Beginning in 1984, fifty Class 303 units received a major refurbishment. One of the main changes was the construction of an internal connecting gangway to permit passage between the three coaches. The vehicles also received new, modern interiors with slide-opening windows being replaced with a more modern hopper design. Most importantly, the dangerous asbestos insulation was also removed. Although the interiors were much brighter and more modern, the seating was not nearly as comfortable as the original deep-sprung seating and many passengers complained that the refurbished Blue Train units had lost their character. Although the destination screen on unit No. 303 069 is set to Ayr, it was very rare to find a Class 303 operating as such.

Class 303 Unit No. 303 082 Vehicle No. 75848

No. 303 082 was one of a number of Class 303 units to be transferred to Manchester Longsight Depot in 1989. Although No. 303 082 has Alderley Edge on her destination screen she is actually back in Scotland and was photographed in Greater Manchester PTE livery at Glasgow Shields Depot, where the Scottish Class 303 units were based. No. 303 082 was un-refurbished and therefore did not re-enter service in Scotland, presumably being used instead as a source of spare parts at this time to help keep the remaining Class 303 units in service.

Class 303 No. 303 087 Vehicle No. 75853

Refurbished No. 303 087 is pictured at Glasgow Central station and is wearing Strathclyde PTE livery. When the Class 303 units were first introduced they featured curved wrap-around windscreens, but following a number of stone-throwing incidents the screens were replaced by toughened flat glass in the 1970s. No. 303 087 was one of only four Class 303 units to receive the later SPT carmine and cream livery.

Class 303 Unidentified Unit

Pictured in the yard at BRML Springburn is an unidentified refurbished Class 303 unit fresh from the paint shop. The Class 303 units were the only Mk 1 based units to feature pneumatically operated sliding passenger doors. Being a refurbished unit, the bright yellow interior applied to these units after refurbishment can be clearly seen through the open doors. A few Class 303 units remained in service as late as 2002, with the last passenger service being recorded as taking place on 30 December 2002 when units Nos 303 011 and 303 088 worked a service to Helensburgh Central.

Class 304 No. 304 006 Vehicle No. 75650

Forty-five Class 304 units were constructed by BR Wolverton Works in 1960. They were originally designated AM4 units before becoming Class 304 units under the TOPS renumbering. They were constructed to operate local services between Manchester, Crewe, Liverpool and Rugby following the electrification of the West Coast Main Line and would remain principally on these lines throughout their working lives. Unit No. 304 006 is pictured passing Manchester Longsight Depot and is painted in BR blue and grey livery. A small number of the Class 304 units would later receive Regional Railways livery before the last of the units were withdrawn and scrapped in 1996.

Class 304 No. 304 035 Vehicle No. 75699

The Class 304 units were similar in appearance to the Class 305 and Class 308 units which were also built around the same time. When delivered, the Class 304 units were originally formed as four-coach units with a Trailer Composite vehicle featuring both first and standard class seating that was arranged in a compartment style layout. In the early 1980s the Trailer Composite vehicles were removed and scrapped. Unit No. 304 035, part of the second batch built, is pictured in BR blue and grey livery, and when this photograph was taken was formed as a three-car unit.

Class 305 No. 305 501 Vehicle No. 75424

The Class 305 units were built by both BR Doncaster and BR York Works in 1960. Originally designated AM5 units, the first fifty-two units built, known as Class 305/1 units, were constructed as three-coach units and featured standard class seating throughout. The next nineteen Class 305 units, known as Class 305/2 units, were constructed as four-coach units with an additional coach – a Trailer Composite containing both standard and first class seating. In the early 1990s most of the Class 305/2 units received Regional Railways livery following overhaul at Doncaster Works. Five Class 305/2 units then moved to Scotrail and operated services on the Edinburgh to North Berwick line. Unit No. 305 501 is pictured in Edinburgh Waverley station wearing Regional Railways livery with Scotrail branding.

Class 305 No. 305 519 Vehicle No. 75461

Unit No. 305 519 was one of five Class 305/2 units that moved to Scotrail in 1992 to operate services on the Edinburgh to North Berwick line. At the time this photograph was taken at Edinburgh Waverley station, she still retained her Network SouthEast livery and her Trailer Standard vehicle had been removed. She did not enter service in this condition and was only in Edinburgh for staff familiarisation of the Class 305/2 units. She would later enter service on the Edinburgh to North Berwick line, by which time she had been reformed back into four-coach formation and received Regional Railways livery.

Class 305 No. 305 527 Vehicle No. 75559

Unit No. 305 527 was originally a three-coach Class 305/1 unit numbered 305 446. Toward the end of the Class 305 units' time in London, a number of Class 305/1 units were refurbished internally and had a Class 302 trailer vehicle added to become a four-coach Class 305/3 unit. The additional vehicles were quickly removed and the refurbished Class 305/3 units returned to being three-coach units. Unit No. 305 527 is pictured at Ilford Depot, having recently been outshopped in Network SouthEast livery. The last Class 305 units were withdrawn around 2001, with all units being scrapped.

Class 306 No. 306 017 Vehicle No. 65217

The Class 306 units were constructed by Metro Cammell and the Birmingham Railway Carriage & Wagon Company in 1949. Ninety-two three-coach units were constructed with all but one unit being withdrawn by the early 1980s. The one remaining unit, No. 306 017, has been preserved at the East Anglian Railway Museum. When the Class 306 units were first constructed they operated on 1,500 V DC. In the 1960s the overhead wires were re-energised at 25 kV AC and the Class 306 units were rebuilt to become compatible with the new electrical supply. Unit No. 306 017 is pictured at Ilford Depot and is looking smart in BR multiple unit green livery.

Class 307 No. 307 102 Vehicle No. 75002

Thirty-two Class 307 units were constructed by BR Eastleigh Works between 1954 and 1956. They were originally designated AM7 units and were similar in design to the Southern Regions Class 415 4EPB units. By 1991 all of the Class 307 units had been withdrawn from London services with most being placed into storage at Kingmoor Yard, Carlisle. However, their days of passenger service were not over just yet, as five units received an overhaul at Doncaster Works. They saw a further two years of service on the Doncaster to Leeds via Wakefield Westgate line until new Class 321/9 units were delivered in 1993. A further three Class 307 units, including unit No. 307 102, were transferred to Yorkshire to facilitate staff training and to possibly provide spare parts. Unit No. 307 102 is pictured at Doncaster station wearing Network SouthEast livery.

Class 307 No. 307 111 Vehicle No. 75011

When the Class 307 units first entered service they were constructed to operate on 1,500 V DC overhead lines. Around 1960 it was decided to upgrade these lines to use 6.25 kV and 25 kV AC current. Therefore, all Class 307 units were sent back to Eastleigh Works, where they were rebuilt to operate on the new voltage. Unit No. 307 111, one of the units later transferred to Yorkshire, is pictured at Wakefield Westgate station operating a West Yorkshire PTE service to Leeds. She is wearing West Yorkshire PTE livery and would be withdrawn by 1993 and placed into storage at MOD Kineton. Later, forty-two Class 307 vehicles were converted by Hunslet Barclay to become Propelling Control Vehicles (PCV) for the Rail Express Systems fleet. The work involved removing the windows, slam doors and fitting roller shutter doors. A PCV could work in push-pull mode with Class 47/7 locomotives and these vehicles remained in service until 2004.

Class 307 No. 307 118 Vehicle No. 75018

Unit No. 307 118 is pictured at Leeds station and is wearing BR blue and grey livery. She was new in 1955 following construction at BR Eastleigh Works. Unit No. 307 118 was later converted to be used as a test train, numbered 316 998, to test new AC traction motors and electrical equipment that was intended to be fitted to new Class 323 units.

Class 308 No. 308 133 Vehicle No. 75878

The Class 308 units were constructed between 1960 and 1961 at BR York Works and were originally designated AM8 units. No. 308 133 is pictured looking smart in Network SouthEast livery at Ilford Depot. The Class 308 units were refurbished between 1981 and 1983, at which time the compartment layout was removed and they were fitted with internal gangways. By the early 1990s, the Class 308s' time in London was coming to an end. In 1994 the line from Leeds to Bradford and Skipton had been electrified and BR decided to refurbish twenty-one Class 308 units to operate on these lines. Following refurbishment at Doncaster Works, they entered service in West Yorkshire PTE red and cream livery. The last Class 308 unit is recorded as being withdrawn in 2001.

Class 309 No. 309 605 Vehicle No. 75988

Twenty-three Class 309 units were constructed by BR York Works between 1962 and 1963 and would become known as 'Clacton Express' units. They were originally designated AM9 units and were formed into either two- or four-coach formation. When first introduced the units operated on services between London Liverpool Street and Clacton-on-Sea and were the first 100 mph EMUs built. Unit No. 309 605 was originally formed with just two coaches but in 1973 she received two additional converted Mk 1 coaches to become a four-coach unit. Unit No. 309 605 is pictured wearing Network SouthEast livery at Ilford Depot.

Class 310 No. 310 109 Vehicle No. 76137

The Class 310 units were built by BR Derby Works between 1965 and 1967. They were originally designated AM10 and were the first EMU units to be based on the Mk 2 coach design. No. 310 109 was originally numbered 310 053 and is pictured wearing Provincial Midline livery. She was withdrawn with the rest of the Class 310/1 units by 2002. Three vehicles from unit No. 310 109, along with vehicle No. 62138 from a Class 423/1 unit, were converted into a test train for Hitachi in 2002, which was numbered 960 201. The unit was known as the Hitachi Verification Train, or V Train, and was used to test Hitachi traction equipment that would later be used within the Class 395 Javelin trains.

Class 310 No. 310 111 Vehicle No. 76147

The Class 310 units were ordered as part of the West Coast Main Line electrification project. They initially operated services between London Euston station and Bletchley, Milton Keynes, Northampton and Birmingham and later worked services on the Great Eastern Main Line from London Liverpool Street station. No. 310 111 was originally numbered 310 063. During refurbishment in 1985 she lost her original curved windscreens and was fitted with flat screens, as can be seen in this photograph of her departing Birmingham New Street station, heading for Coventry, while wearing Provincial Midline livery.

Class 311 No. 311 104 Vehicle No. 76415

Nineteen Class 311 units were constructed in 1967, intended for use on the newly electrified Inverclyde lines from Glasgow Central to Gourock and Wemyss Bay. Although very similar to the Class 303 units, which were built by Pressed Steel in 1960, the Class 311 units were constructed to an earlier Mk 1 design by Craven of Sheffield. All of the Class 311 units were withdrawn in the 1990s, long before the last of the Class 303 units were withdrawn. Only a handful of Class 311 units received Strathclyde PTE livery, but none were refurbished. Unit No. 311 104 is pictured in BR blue and grey livery at Edinburgh Waverley station in 1991. The final two Class 311 units, Nos 311 103 and 311 104, became Class 936 sandite units, which remained in service until 1999. Unit No. 936 104, formerly No. 311 104, was scrapped in 2003.

Class 312 No. 312 799 Vehicle No. 76993

The Class 312 units were constructed by BR York Works between 1976 and 1978. Forty-nine four-coach units were constructed and they were originally designated as AM12 units. They were the last slam-door EMUs constructed and were also the last EMUs built using the Mk 2 bodyshell. The units were similar in appearance to the Class 310 units, but were fitted with flat windscreens from new and were capable of 90 mph. No. 312 799 is pictured wearing Network SouthEast livery in a dark London Liverpool Street station when getting ready to depart to Ipswich. The last members of the Class 312 fleet were withdrawn in June 2004.

Class 313 No. 313 001 Vehicle No. 62593

The Class 313 units were the first of the second generation EMU units to be built. Sixty-four three-coach units were constructed by BR York Works between February 1976 and April 1977. The units featured air-operated sliding passenger doors and new Tightlock couplers, which enabled the driver to couple and un-couple from the driving cab. The passenger doors were originally operated by the passengers using a handle, which caused problems when the passengers opened the doors before the train was at a stand. The handles were later changed for push buttons. No. 313 001 is pictured departing from London Euston station and is heading for Willesden Junction. She originally wore BR blue and grey livery but by the time this photograph was taken she was wearing Network SouthEast livery and would later receive Silverlink livery. Unit No. 313 001 is now numbered 313 201 and currently carries Southern Rail Coastway livery.

Class 313 No. 313 020 No. Vehicle 62612

Unit No. 313 020 is pictured heading to Welwyn Garden City, Hertfordshire. She would become No. 313 220 after refurbishment and currently operates Southern Coastway services from Brighton while wearing Southern Coastway livery. The Class 313 units were dual voltage units and able to operate on both 25 kV AV and 750 V DC lines. They were also designed to operate over London Underground Tube lines between Drayton Park and Moorgate station, and therefore featured a lower roof profile and end gangway doors that were for emergency use only. The Class 313 units, now over forty years old, are due to be replaced by new Class 717 units in 2018.

Class 314 No. 314 210 Vehicle No. 64601

In 1979, BR York Works constructed sixteen Class 314 units for Strathclyde PTE services via the newly reopened Argyle line in Glasgow. No. 314 210 is pictured at Partick station, heading for Dalmuir, and is wearing Strathclyde PTE livery. The units were originally delivered in BR blue and grey livery. They later received Strathclyde PTE orange and black livery and SPT carmine and cream livery following that. Many units now carry Scotrail Saltire livery and can still be found operating services from Glasgow Central High Level station.

Class 314 No. 314 213 Vehicle No. 64607

The Argyle line services stretched as far as Lanark and often Class 314 units could be found working services via the West Coast Main Line to this destination. No. 314 213 is pictured approaching the junction for Lanark at Cleghorn level crossing on the West Coast Main Line. Since 2002 the units have operated services from Glasgow Central High Level station to Newton, Neilston and the Cathcart Circle. Occasionally the units can be found working Inverclyde services but not having been fitted with on-board toilets means that they are unsuitable for longer journeys. Since November 2012, and following electrification of the line, the Class 314 units have taken over operation of the Glasgow Central to Paisley Canal line services from Class 156 units.

Class 314 No. 314 215 Vehicle No. 64611

The Class 314 units contained two motor coaches, both driving vehicles and one trailer vehicle, which was fitted with the pantograph. No. 314 215 is pictured heading towards Lanark on the West Coast Main Line. She is wearing Strathclyde PTE livery and would later receive SPT carmine and cream livery. The gangway end door was fitted to all PEP type units (Class 313, Class 314, Class 315, Class 507 and Class 508) but was for emergency use only.

Class 314 Unidentified Unit

An unidentified Class 314 unit is pictured undergoing overhaul within BRML Springburn Works. Although her destination screen is set to Ayr, it was very rare for these units to operate services on the Ayrshire lines. Class 314 unit No. 314 203 was involved in a fatal accident at Newton Junction on 21 July 1991 wherein the leading coach, No. 64588, was completely destroyed. The remaining two coaches were placed into storage for a few years but a Class 507 vehicle from Merseyside was later converted to a 25 kV AC vehicle and set No. 314 203 was reformed. Interestingly, the converted Class 507 vehicle lost its original fleet number, 64426, and received the number of the earlier destroyed vehicle, 64588. The 'new' No. 64588 vehicle was also fitted with experimental seating around the same time.

Class 315 No. 315 848 Vehicle No. 64556

The Class 315 units were the final PEP type units built and were constructed by BR York Works between 1980 and 1981. Sixty-one Class 315 units were constructed. No. 315 848 is pictured at Ilford Depot and is wearing Network SouthEast livery. She would later receive National Express livery, followed by Abellio Greater Anglia livery. Since 2015 she has been part of TfL Rail, operating Shenfield Metro services, and she now carries TfL Rail's blue and white livery.

Class 315 No. 315 855 Vehicle No. 64570

No. 315 855 is pictured at London Liverpool Street station. She is wearing Network SouthEast livery but also has had a BR logo fitted next to the crew door. No. 315 855 was delivered in BR blue and grey livery before receiving Network SouthEast livery. She later carried both National Express ONE livery and National Express livery and has also carried two versions of the TfL Rail livery. She currently wears TfL blue and white livery and operates Shenfield Metro services for TfL. The future of the units is uncertain since both London Overground and TfL Rail have new Class 345 and Class 710 units on order that are intended to replace the Class 315 units.

Class 316 No. 316 998 Vehicle No. 75018

Unit No. 316 998 began life in 1954 as a Class 307 unit numbered 307 118. Upon withdrawal from service she became a test bed for new traction motors that were intended to be used in new Class 323 units. She is pictured attending an open day event while numbered 316 998 and is wearing BR blue livery. She would later go on to become a further test bed unit, numbered 316 997 and this time operating over 750 V DC lines. Upon withdrawal she was placed into storage at Eastleigh Depot and is recorded as being scrapped in 2006.

Class 317 No. 316 326 Vehicle No. 77025

The Class 317 units were the first electric units to be constructed using the Mk 3 bodyshell and were constructed by BREL at York between 1981 and 1987. They were constructed in two batches. The first forty-eight units were known as Class 317/1 units and were constructed between 1981 and 1982. Between 1985 and 1987 a further twenty-four units were constructed and were designated Class 317/2 units. Unit No. 317 326 is pictured wearing Network SouthEast livery at London St Pancras station. Following refurbishment in 2006 she emerged from Doncaster Works as unit No. 317 884. The Class 317/2 units featured a restyled, more rounded front end and larger hopper windows. The location of the photograph has changed dramatically, with the station now becoming the terminal station for Eurostar services.

Class 318 No. 318 250 Vehicle No. 77260

Unit No. 318 250 was the first of twenty-one Class 318 units to be constructed at BREL York Works between 1985 and 1986. They were ordered for the newly electrified Ayrshire lines and entered service in September 1986. She is pictured on a sunny day at Platform 1 of Largs station and is wearing Strathclyde PTE orange and black livery. In July 1995 unit No. 318 254 experienced brake failure when approaching Platform 1 at Largs station and smashed through the station building, coming to rest on the street outside the station. Thankfully, being an early morning service, there were no serious injuries. The station took many years to be rebuilt but sadly lost much of its glass canopy.

Class 318 No. 318 266 Vehicle No. 77256

Unit No. 318 266 is pictured fresh from the paint shop at BRML Springburn Works, Glasgow. She is looking smart in Strathclyde PTE orange and black livery and like her sisters would later receive SPT carmine and cream livery followed by Scotrail Saltire livery. Vehicle No. 77256 carried the name *Strathclyder* for many years and is recorded as being de-named following overhaul in January 2016. The author was signed for Class 318 units and operated them for many years on Ayrshire services before they were replaced by new Class 380 units.

Class 318 No. 318 270 Vehicle No. 77288

Driving Trailer vehicle No. 77288 is pictured at BRML Springburn Works, Glasgow, in Strathclyde PTE orange and black livery. She has been separated from the rest of the unit while she undergoes accident repair work. The Class 318 units were refurbished between 2005 and 2007 at Hunslet Barclay, Kilmarnock. During this refurbishment the units lost their end gangway doors but received new cab windows along with a repaint into SPT carmine and cream livery. All Class 318 units now carry Scotrail Saltire livery.

Class 319 No. 319 008 Vehicle No. 77304

The Class 319 units were constructed by BREL at their York Works between 1987 and 1990. The Class 319 units were ordered to operate services on the newly opened Thameslink Bedford to Brighton route. As the Thameslink line was electrified using 25 kV AC overhead wires north of Farringdon, and 750 V DC third rail south of Farringdon, the units were required to be dual voltage and be able to switch between both supplies. No. 319 008 is pictured in Network SouthEast livery. On 10 December 1993 she carried the first British passengers through the Channel Tunnel to France. She received the name *Cheriton* and was also fitted with a plaque commemorating the event, which featured both British and French flags. Unit No. 319 008 was withdrawn and placed into storage at Long Marston on 21 July 2017.

Class 319 No. 319 050 Vehicle No. 77437

Class 319 unit No. 319 050 is pictured at London Kings Cross Thameslink station. This station closed on 8 December 2007 when the new King Cross St Pancras Thameslink station opened beneath London St Pancras International station. The Class 319 units featured an end gangway door, which was fitted as an emergency exit since the units would operate through the single-bore Smithfield Tunnel. Following refurbishment at Railcare Wolverton in 1997, unit No. 319 050 became unit No. 319 450. Thirty-two Class 319 units, including unit No. 319 450, are now allocated to Northern Rail and operate services over electrified lines around the North West area. All Class 319 units have now been withdrawn from Thameslink services and have been replaced by new Class 700 units.

Class 320 No. 320 304 Vehicle No. 77902

Twenty-two Class 320 units were constructed by BREL York Works in 1990. They all entered service in the Strathclyde area and were ordered to replace the elderly Class 303 and Class 311 units, which were approaching thirty years old. They first entered service on the North Clyde line and could regularly be found calling at Partick station, where this photograph of No. 320 304 was taken. The Class 320 units later received SPT carmine and cream livery and now carry Scotrail Saltire livery. The Class 320 units were effectively three-coach Class 321 units, with the centre trailing vehicle removed. Unfortunately, the vehicle omitted from the Class 320 units was the coach that would have contained the toilet. This was rectified between 2011 and 2013, when all Class 320 units were fitted with a fully accessible toilet.

Class 320 No. 320 317 Vehicle No. 77937

The Class 320 units were restricted to a maximum speed of 75 mph as they were built without yaw dampers being fitted. It had not been felt necessary to specify yaw dampers due to the suburban work the units were ordered for. In 2010 all Class 320 units were finally fitted with yaw dampers, which permitted their maximum speed to increase in line with the Class 318 units that they regularly worked alongside to 90 mph. A nearly new Class 320 unit, No. 320 317 is pictured at High Street station operating a service to Airdrie. In December 2010 the line from Airdrie was reopened to Bathgate, which then permitted trains to run from Glasgow Queen Street Low Level station to Edinburgh Waverley station via Airdrie and Bathgate.

Class 321 No. 321 338 Vehicle No. 77890

Between 1988 and 1991, 117 Class 321 units were constructed by BREL at their York Works. No. 321 338 is pictured in Network SouthEast livery at Ilford Depot. The 'P' code added at the end of the fleet number denotes that this end of the unit is fitted with a lockable parcels area that is located in the area between the cab and the leading set of passenger doors. The Class 321 units entered service on the Great Eastern Main Line and replaced earlier Class 305, Class 308 and Class 309 units. After carrying Network SouthEast livery for many years, she later received First Great Eastern livery and now carries Abellio Greater Anglia livery.

Class 321 No. 321 402 Vehicle No. 77944

Representing the second batch of Class 321 units is No. 321 402, which is pictured in Network SouthEast livery at London Euston station when getting ready to depart for Northampton. The small panel that can be seen next to the door-control buttons on the rear coach would light up to inform passengers that this area of the coach is locked and out of use when being used for parcel traffic. In 2010, unit No. 321 402 was one of thirteen Class 321/4 units to be transferred to First Capital Connect services. Later, in 2017, she would pass to Abellio Greater Anglia, where she now operates in de-branded First Group livery. The future is uncertain for many of the Class 321 units as Abellio Greater Anglia has placed an order for new Class 720 units, which are intended to replace many Class 317 and Class 321 units.

Class 321 No. 321 902 Vehicle No. 77994

The final batch of Class 321s, designated Class 321/9s, numbered just three units. They were constructed by BREL at their York Works in 1991 but did not fully enter service on the line between Doncaster and Leeds until 1993. A nearly new Class 321/9 unit, numbered 321 902, is pictured at Doncaster station, looking smart in West Yorkshire PTE red and cream livery. Unlike the Class 321/3 and Class 321/4 units, the Class 321/9 units were not fitted with first class seating.

Class 322 No. 322 481 Vehicle No. 77985

The Class 322 units were the final multiple units to be constructed by BREL that were based on the Mk 3 bodyshell. Five units were constructed by BREL at York Works in 1990 and were ordered to operate services between London Liverpool Street station and Stansted Airport, which opened in 1991. No. 321 481 is pictured at London Liverpool Street station and is wearing Stanstead Express livery. She would later move to Scotland in 2001 and operated services between Edinburgh Waverley station and North Berwick until approximately 2010. During this time she carried First Scotrail livery and the name *North Berwick Flyer 1850 – 2000*. Following her time in Scotland she headed south and entered service with Northern Rail alongside the rest of the Class 322 units on services around the Leeds area.

Class 322 No. 322 482 Vehicle No. 78164

Class 321 482 is pictured at London Liverpool Street station and has just arrived from Stansted Airport. In 2001, unit No. 322 482 transferred north to Scotland and later received First Scotrail livery. She could be found operating services between Edinburgh Waverley and North Berwick until around 2010. The Class 322 units replaced the older Class 305 unit, which had operated on this line for a few years following electrification. Following their time in Scotland the Class 322 units were transferred to Northern Rail and are due to be replaced with new Class 331 units in 2019.

Class 411 No. 1577 Vehicle No. 61719

The Class 411 units were constructed at BR Eastleigh Works between 1956 and 1963. A total of 111 units were constructed and were known as 4CEP units. A further twenty-two similar 4BEP units, later designated Class 410 units, were also constructed and had a Buffet vehicle in place of one of the Trailer Standard vehicles fitted to the 4CEP units. No. 1577 is pictured at London Victoria station. She is wearing two-tone brown and orange London & South Eastern livery, known as Jaffa Cake livery, and she later received Network SouthEast livery. The majority of the Class 411 units were withdrawn around 2003 with a few units remaining in traffic until 2005, by which time they were forty-nine years old.

Class 414 No. 4315 Vehicle No. 75415

Class 414 unit No. 4315 was a 2HAP unit which was constructed in 1959 at BR Eastleigh Works. The 2HAP units were built in three batches between 1956 and 1963, with a total of 209 units being built. Withdrawal of the units began in 1982 and the final Class 414 unit was withdrawn in 1995. A number of Driving Brake vehicles (DMBSO) from withdrawn Class 414 units were converted to become Class 489 GLV vehicles for use on Gatwick Express services. Class 414 unit 4315 is pictured in Network SouthEast livery and was withdrawn shortly after this photograph was taken in 1992.

Class 415 No. 5408 Unidentified Vehicle

The Class 415 units were constructed by Eastleigh Works between 1951 and 1961. Units built between 1951 and 1957 were based on an upgraded Class 405 Southern Railway design but featured electro-pneumatic brakes, which led to the Class 415 units being known as 4EPB units. Later-built units were constructed to a British Rail design based on the Mk 1 coach. Class 415 unit No. 5408 is pictured looking smart in Network SouthEast livery. The last Class 415 units were withdrawn in 1995, having been replaced by Class 455, Class 456, Class 465 and Class 466 units.

Class 415 No. 5468 Vehicle No. 14212

Class 415 unit No. 5468 is pictured in BR blue and grey livery at London Charing Cross station. Many Class 415 units later received Network SouthEast livery. However, No. 5468 was not one and was withdrawn from service by 1993. She has, however, been fitted with Network SouthEast and Kent Link logos. The Class 415 units were capable of 75 mph, with a few units latterly being re-geared to give a top speed of 90 mph.

Class 416 No. 6417 Vehicle No. 65366

A total of 128 Class 416 units were built at Eastleigh Works between 1953 and 1956 and were two-coach units known as 2EPB units. The majority of the Class 416 units were constructed to operate London suburban services but fifteen Class 416 units were built in 1954 to operate services between Newcastle and South Shields. In 1963 BR decided to withdraw electric traction in Tyneside and these units were redeployed to operate on South London services. Class 416 unit No. 6417 was one of twenty-six Class 416 units that became Class 416/4 units in 1986 following refurbishment, and she is pictured here at London Charing Cross station. The last of the Class 416 units would be withdrawn from service in 1995 replaced by new Class 456 units.

Class 422 No. 2254 Vehicle No. 76803

The Class 422 units, known as 4BIG units, were similar to the Class 421 4CIG units. In total, 138 Class 421 units and twenty-eight Class 422 units were built between 1964 and 1972 at BR York Works. Although similar in design, Class 422 units were fitted with a buffet coach while Class 421 units contained an extra standard class coach. The units were refurbished between 1986 and 1993 and remained in service until 2005, with two units operating services on the Lymington Branch until 2010. Class 422 unit No. 2254 is pictured wearing Network SouthEast livery and, at the time this photograph was taken, she has lost her buffet coach. No. 69306 can be found on the Spa Valley Railway and is in use as a static café at Tunbridge Wells station.

Class 438 No. 8014 Vehicle No. 76296

Class 438 unit No. 8014 is pictured at Sheffield station on 29 September 1990. She had formed part of a railtour from Eastleigh to Sheffield in connection with an open day event at the nearby Tinsley Depot. The Class 438 units were four-coach, unpowered units that were converted from Mk 1 coaches by BR York Works between 1966 and 1967. Known as 4TC units, they would normally be found on the London Waterloo to Weymouth line. Being unpowered, they would normally be propelled from London to Bournemouth by a 4REP unit over electrified lines, and then be hauled from Bournemouth to Weymouth using a Class 33/1 locomotive. The Class 438 units would be replaced on the London to Bournemouth and Weymouth line by new Class 442 units from 1988 onwards. Unit No. 8014 would be withdrawn shortly after this photograph was taken in September 1990, in which she is seen still wearing BR blue and grey livery.

Class 442 No. 2403 Vehicle No. 77384

The Class 442 units were constructed at BREL Derby Works in 1988 and were based on the BR Mk 3 coach. They entered service between London Waterloo and Bournemouth/Weymouth lines and replaced the Class 438 units. They were known as Wessex Electrics but many enthusiasts also gave them the nickname Plastic Pigs due to their curved plastic front ends. The Class 442 units continued to operate express services from London Waterloo station until February 2007, when they were replaced by modern Class 444 and Class 450 units. Following a brief period in storage at Eastleigh, most re-entered service, where they were used to operate Gatwick Express services. After a further nine years the Class 442 units were again withdrawn and placed into storage at Ely Papworth sidings. Class 442 unit No. 2403 is pictured arriving into London Waterloo station. No. 2403 was placed in storage at Ely on 28 October 2016.

Class 442 No. 2411 Vehicle No. 77392

Class 442 unit No. 2411 is pictured at Clapham Junction Depot while wearing Network SouthEast livery. Like the rest of the Class 442 units, she was withdrawn and placed into storage at Eastleigh in 2007 before re-entering service in 2008 on Gatwick Express services. She was again withdrawn in 2016 and moved to storage at Ely Papworth sidings on 18 November 2016. The Class 442 units were capable of 100 mph, with one unit setting a world speed record for a third rail train of 108 mph on 11 April 1988. The Class 442 units featured metal lids below the windscreens, which were designed to improve the appearance of the units by covering the various pipes and cables used for multiple working. These lids were heavy and were often removed, as can be seen on the previous photograph. Currently, all Class 442 units are withdrawn, although plans are in place that could see eighteen of the twenty-four units re-enter service on London Waterloo to Portsmouth services in 2018.

Class 455 No. 5729 Vehicle No. 77784

The Class 455 units were constructed in three batches at BREL York Works between 1982 and 1985. Unit No. 5729 was one of forty-three Class 455/7 units that formed part of the second batch that was built. When the Class 455 units first entered service on South London lines, they permitted the older Class 508 units to be transferred to Merseyside, where they were originally planned to operate. Before the Class 508 units headed north, their centre trailer vehicle (TSO) was removed and added to the formation of the new Class 455/7 units. Class 455 729 is pictured at East Wimbledon Depot. The second coach from the camera is numbered 71550 and is the TSO vehicle that has been added to the unit from a Class 508 unit. The difference in body profile between the two types of coaches used in the formation can be clearly seen in this photograph.

Class 455 No. 5735 Vehicle No. 77795

Class 455/7 unit No. 5735 is pictured at London Waterloo station. The Class 455/7 units were actually constructed after the Class 455/8 units and featured the revised front end styling as applied to the later Class 317 and Class 318 units. Although similar in appearance to both Class 317 and Class 318 units, the Class 455 were not fitted with toilets and had a top speed of 75 mph, reflecting their intended use on suburban services. The Class 455 units are due to be replaced by Class 701 Aventra units in December 2019.

Class 455 No. 5853 Vehicle No. 77683

The first Class 455 units constructed were seventy-four Class 455/8 units, which were built by BREL at York Works between 1982 and 1984. Like the first batch of Class 317 units constructed, the Class 455/8 units featured a squarer front end and different headlight units compared with the later Class 455 units. Class 455 unit No. 5853 is pictured at East Wimbledon Depot. The Class 455 units first entered service in BR blue and grey livery before receiving Network SouthEast livery. Unit No. 5853 also carried a red all-over advertising livery for Côtes du Rhône around 2002. A total of 137 Class 455 units were constructed between 1982 and 1985 and all entered service on South London suburban lines.

Class 456 No. 456 010 Vehicle No. 64744

Twenty-four Class 456 units were constructed by BREL at York Works between 1990 and 1991. They were ordered as a replacement for the Class 416 2EPB units, which dated from 1953. Although Network SouthEast had introduced a revised livery featuring a lighter shade of grey, the Class 456 units were delivered in the original, darker livery. This was to ensure the units matched the livery that the earlier Class 455 units carried as it was intended that the Class 456 units would work in multiple with the Class 455 units. No. 456 010 is pictured at Strawberry Hill Depot shortly after delivery from York.

Class 456 No. 456 020 Vehicle No. 64754

The Class 456 units featured the same cab design as the Class 320, Class 321 and Class 322 units. When first delivered it was found that, due to the design of the cab, the drivers were unable to view the platform monitors when operating in driver-only mode. The Class 456 units were placed into storage for approximately ten months from new at Strawberry Hill Depot until a modification to the driver's seat was introduced, which overcame the viewing problem. This photograph of unit No. 456 020 was taken at Strawberry Hill Depot during the time the units were in storage.

Class 465 No. 456 003 Unidentified Vehicle

The Class 465 units, known as Networker units, were constructed between 1991 and 1994 and were intended to replace the Class 415 units that dated from 1951. In total 147 units were constructed in three batches. The Class 465/0 and Class 465/1 units, totalling ninety-seven, were constructed at York Works by BREL, and latterly by ABB. The Class 465/2 units, which numbered fifty, were constructed by Metro-Cammell between 1991 and 1993. Although visually very similar, the York-built units featured different traction equipment to the Class 465/2 units. Unit No. 465 003 is pictured in the new, brighter Network SouthEast livery while awaiting entry into service. She would later receive Connex South Eastern livery and now carries Southeastern livery.

Class 465 No. 456 005 Vehicle No. 64763

No. 465 005 was constructed at BREL York Works in 1991. The Class 465 units featured regenerative braking and had a maximum speed of 75 mph, which suited their suburban operation. No. 465 005 is pictured attending an open day event at Eastleigh Depot on 27 September 1992. Over the years she has worn Network SouthEast livery, Connex South Eastern and finally Southeastern livery.

Class 487 Vehicle No. 53

The Class 487 vehicles were constructed by English Electric in 1940 for the operation of the Waterloo & City line, which opened in 1898. They were replaced with modern Class 482 units in 1992, with the line later passing to London Transport in 1994. The units did not run in fixed formations and trains would usually be formed with a mixture of motor and trailer vehicles. A total of twelve driving motor vehicles and sixteen trailer vehicles were constructed. Driving motor vehicle No. 53 is pictured upon arrival at London Waterloo Station. The Class 487 vehicles did not receive yellow front end warning panels since the line was self-contained, operating within a tunnel. Following withdrawal of the Class 487 vehicles, one vehicle, No. 61, can be found within the London Transport Acton collection, having been recently restored in Network SouthEast livery.

Class 504 No. 504 447 Vehicle No. 65447

The Class 504 units were constructed by BR Wolverton Works in 1959 to operate the Manchester Victoria to Bury line. Twenty-six units were built and were formed of two coaches – a Driving Motor Brake coach and a Driving Trailer coach. Unit numbers were never carried but the individual vehicle number was always displayed on the front end, as seen in this picture of No. 65447, which is arriving into Bury station. The Class 504 units were unique and operated on a 1,200 V DC third rail supply. Interestingly, the traction power would pass to the Class 504 units from the electrified rail using side contact equipment rather than conventional equipment that would use a collection shoe in contact with the top of the live rail. The final units were withdrawn in 1991, when the line closed.

Class 504 No. 504 447 Vehicle No. 65447

Another view of No. 504 447, this time taken at the opposite end of the line at Manchester Victoria station. She is pictured wearing Greater Manchester PTE livery, which was carried by all Class 504 units that remained in service when the line closed in 1991. Following closure the line was converted to light rail and became the first section of the Manchester Metrolink. The location of this photograph has changed dramatically following the conversion of the line to Metrolink, with the units now passing through the station, across Corporation Street and through the city centre to Piccadilly Gardens.

Class 508 No. 508 113 Unidentified Vehicle

The Class 508 units were constructed by BR York Works between 1979 and 1980. They initially entered service on South London lines and following the delivery of new Class 455/7 units between 1982 and 1985, the Class 508 units transferred to the Merseyside area. Before they headed north, the Class 508 units had one of their centre trailer vehicles removed, which was added to the formation of the Class 455/7 units. They were also renumbered to become units Nos 508 101 to 508 143. Unit No. 508 113 is pictured at Hooton station – the limit of the electrification of the Wirral line at this time. Unit No. 508 113 was one of twelve Class 508 units that were transferred back to the London area in 1996 and, following refurbishment, she received fleet number 508 206. Following withdrawal in 2008 she is recorded as being scrapped at Eastleigh in 2013.

Class 930 No. 005 Vehicle No. ADB 975588

Unit No. 005 was a departmental unit that began life as a Class 405 unit numbered 4121. Vehicle No. ADB 975588 was previously numbered 10981. A total of 185 Class 405 units, known as 4SUB units, were built at Eastleigh Works between 1941 and 1951. Unit No. 005 was one of thirteen Class 405 units to be converted to de-icing and sandite units in 1979. She is pictured in the yard at East Wimbledon Depot and is recorded as being withdrawn and scrapped in 2003.

Class 931 No. 062 Vehicle No. ADB 977560

Unit No. 062 was converted from two Class 416 units in 1987 to become a departmental unit. She was used to deliver carriage-cleaning fluid, de-icer and other liquids around the Network SouthEast area. Known as the 'NSE Liquid Delivery Unit' or 'The Sprinkler', she began life in 1954 as one of the fifteen Class 416 units that were constructed at Eastleigh Works for services in South Tyneside. The units later moved south to the London area in 1963 and remained in service until 1985. Unit No. 062 was withdrawn in 2002 and, after a period in storage at Ramsgate Depot, she was scrapped at Immingham in 2004.